Those Were The Days
Buckinghamshire
in the Forties, Fifties and Sixties

Compiled by
Buckinghamshire Federation
of Women's Institutes

Published jointly by
COUNTRYSIDE BOOKS, Newbury,
and the BFWI, High Wyc

COUNTRYSIDE BOOKS
3 Catherine Road
Newbury, Berkshire

To view our complete range of books,
please visit us at
www.countrysidebooks.co.uk

ISBN 1 85306 710 5

Designed by Roger Davis, K.D.P. Kingsclere
Produced through MRM Associates Ltd., Reading
Typeset by Techniset Typesetters, Newton-le-Willows
Printed by Woolnough Bookbinding Ltd., Irthlingborough

CONTENTS

FOREWORD

As a relative newcomer who came to Buckinghamshire at the end of the period reviewed in this book, I have been enthralled by its anecdotes and content.

The villages were different then, not only in Buckinghamshire but over the country at large. For those who spent some part of their life in the times and places depicted in this book, it is difficult now to appreciate that changes over the last thirty years have been of such magnitude as to almost obliterate the memory of those times.

As we begin a new century, it is important to record how things were so very different – where the telephone was still a novelty in the villages and the red call box was the only means of immediate communication for most people – where the television was only black and white with one channel – where many houses had no bathroom and only a communal privy at the bottom of the garden.

During the 1940s the war created great deprivation and anxiety for many country people and the recollection of the era was probably more romantic than the reality. The memories are of a more relaxed age when horses still ploughed the fields, binders cut the corn, the threshing machines did their village rounds some powered by steam engines, children could walk to school and all the village was able to conduct its life in relative safety.

The Buckinghamshire Women's Institute members who have contributed material for this book seek to preserve the spirit of these times and the comradeship within the community they lived in. We hope new generations will reflect upon this important part of our recent history and contemplate what life may be like some thirty to sixty years on.

Ann Spalton
Federation Chairman
Buckinghamshire Federation of Women's Institutes

CHAPTER ONE
WARTIME MEMORIES

'One afternoon my grandfather and I were feeding chickens, when the air raid siren sounded. We heard a noise overhead, and saw a German plane come low over the field, the pilot looking out at us, with a pleasant look on his face. A moment I will never forget.'

(June Mapley – Water Eaton)

As the Forties began, England was engaged in a fight for survival. Since 3rd September 1939 we had been at war with Germany, and six long years were to pass before we could greet Peace with street parties and bonfire celebrations. In the meantime we were liable, as June Mapley discovered as a child, to encounter the enemy in our very own backyard.

Buckinghamshire was not a front-line county, but even here the threat from bombs, incendiary devices and, later the doodlebugs was an unpleasant and sometimes frightening reality. Children grappled with problems unknown to previous generations. 'We had regular gas mask drill and I shall always remember the look of compassion on the teacher's face when she fitted the horrid stifling thing on me,' recalled *Irene Smith (Winslow).*

Prudence Goodwin (Wingrave) had memories of 'travelling home on the bus, counting the people in the queue because only so many were allowed to stand and if you were left behind the next bus would be at least another hour. All the depressing black-out curtains ... the sticky tape criss-crossed over the windows ... watching the incendiary bombs falling ... hearing the siren and sitting under the kitchen table until the all clear and being aware that Mummy was anxious.'

Her mother was right to be anxious, as Prudence went on. 'The noise and sight of a flying bomb passing over very low as we walked back to school after the dinner hour remains with me to this day. Everybody ran out of their houses, saucepan in hand, screaming "lay down, lay down". It landed in the next village on the school, killing two teachers, the children spared because like us they were not in school.'

Grace King (Wingrave) pointed out the rather antiquated method of raising the alarm in the villages. 'Mr Stubbs who was headmaster of the village school, was also an air raid warden, and if there was an air raid warning he would ride around the village on his bicycle blowing his whistle in short, sharp blasts to let people know that there could be enemy aircraft in the vicinity. When the danger was passed, Mr Stubbs would then cycle round again blowing long blasts on his whistle, indicating the all clear. Over a period of time we had two land mines, two bombs and dozens of incendiaries dropped.'

'In November 1940, German planes on their way to bomb Coventry passed over Hanslope,' recalled *Barbara Bellham (Hanslope)*. 'I vividly remember sleeping on a mattress under the stairs. During the month that this took place bombs were dropped in our street and, although little damage was done, the memory remains clear.'

Even where there was no risk to life, bombs caused damage over a wide area, as *Mrs M. Sears (Radnage)* found out. 'On 13th October 1941 a flying bomb fell in a field in the valley, below our home. This resulted in two cows and a donkey being killed and as the blast came up the fields and over our home, it fetched the ceilings down. In those days they were lath and plaster. We also found the back door in pieces on the mat, and it cracked the cement in our rainwater tank. My husband (he was in the fire service) had to go down and re-do the whole lot. The coalman brought a container with 1,000 gallons of water in it (we paid 2s 6d) and put it in the tank. We used to pump the water up to a cistern in the roof, and 20 minutes pumping time would last a day. The ceilings in the council houses in Radnage were cracked all the way round. The bomb was in the field below the council houses.'

The flying bombs, in particular were a terrifying weapon because though they could be seen and heard, it was not always possible to be sure where they would land. 'In 1944 at the age of twelve, I went on a school camp holiday to Great Kimble from my home in Holmer Green. One night a V1 flying bomb (a doodlebug, as the Londoners called them) landed two fields away from us. I can remember hearing the thud and feeling the vibrations. We were then allowed to double up in our tents for the rest of the night. Meanwhile back in Holmer Green, the V1 bomb had been seen heading in our direction, which obviously caused much concern for all back home.' *(Jean Clarke, Princes Risborough Evening)*

'The village of Coleshill, near Amersham, fared quite well in the war,' reckoned *Lindsey Haubner (Coleshill)*. 'There was a searchlight, manned by a detachment of the Royal Engineers, positioned in the cricket meadow in the early part of the war, as this was the second highest point in the Chilterns. This became a target for bombs but, despite a huge 1,000 lb-er, which didn't explode and a few incendiaries which all landed on farmland, no structural damage or human injury occurred there or anywhere in the village. The 1,000 lb bomb went in 30 feet deep and a steamer was used to defuse it before it could be dug out.

'There was a large army camp built in Hodgemoor Woods, which housed regiments including the 51st Division of the Highland Regiment and the Middlesex Regiment. After the war, the camp was used to house a large number of Polish refugees who had helped us during the conflict but were now homeless. Quite a large Polish community flourished there and links with the village have remained.'

MY FIRST JOB

Those who worked on the 'Home Front' during the war were making almost as great a contribution to the war effort as the fighting forces, by keeping services and businesses going. But actually getting to and from work was sometimes hazardous in itself, as *Betty Wells (Taplow & Hitcham)* recalled.

'In late 1939 I started my first job on the trading estate in Slough, which at that time was in Bucks.

'The most difficult aspect was transport. You could manage to get to the office on time (standing), but getting home could be something of a lottery. Buses that started in Slough were more often than not full by the time they reached the estate and that was cramming in as many as they could. This was later helped by starting some buses from the estate, which was wonderful when they turned up and the weather was clear, but come the fog (and there was a lot at that time) it was a different story.

'I remember one occasion on a very foggy night, pitch black, in early 1940. The buses were conspicuous by their absence. Rather than wait in the cold and dark, I decided to walk home (four and a half miles) to Maidenhead, a bit of an ordeal by yourself in the blackout. But I sang (badly) to myself to keep my

No need to let yourself go — hand cream was available 'through Chemists, Stores and NAAFI'.

spirits up, to arrive home very tired and really rather miserable, to be greeted by my mother with "And where have you been?" I then dissolved into tears, relieved to be home safe at last.

'If you caught the bus before 8.30 am the fare was 7d, after that time it was 9d. But as I started work at the magnificent wage of 17s 6d a week, I did my best to get the early bus.

'On one occasion I was working by myself when I was startled to hear anti-aircraft fire and on looking out of the window was staggered to see a plane with a swastika fly by at roof top height with tracer bullets all around. They all missed!

'Later on, in 1944 I was working at a branch of my firm in Cressex, at that time in the middle of fields, when the skies were filled with the sound of planes. Then from all directions came an armada of gliders being towed, the sky was completely filled with them. We all naturally wondered where they were going and why. We soon found out they were on their way to Arnhem. It is something that will live in my memory for ever.'

BRINGING UP A FAMILY

Babies continued to arrive, and family life to be lived, war or no war. The late *Kathleen Wiffen (Terriers & Totteridge and Penn & Tylers Green)* set down her memories of wartime life as a young mother.

'Our elder daughter was born on 29th December 1942. I waited for her all Christmas Day, eating peppermints which somehow seemed quite necessary for my wellbeing. She was a bonny baby in spite of all the rationing of food. Even nappies were rationed (and no such thing as disposable ones). One bonus was that Baby had a full allowance of tea coupons, a welcome bartering commodity. We lived near Bomber Command and saw Bomber Harris in his car most days.

'One night when raids were particularly bad, we were all downstairs sleeping in front of the fire when my aunt said to me, "I am sorry to disturb you Kath, but there is a bomb coming down" and sure enough we soon heard the whistle and crunches. They fell in a field near us, and one just behind our house down the cesspit.

'I used to push Baby's pram three miles into Wycombe to do the shopping and then home again. The huge Churchill tanks used to leave Broom and Wades and trundle up the valley past the park to practise on Downley Common. There was no footpath in those days. I heard them start off and had to run in order to pull into the park gates leading to the church. The noise trapped down the valley was terrifying and deafening and used to make Baby scream. They used to keep an old billy goat in the park and you could smell him half a mile away. He used to graze on his knees.

'My mother often had the baby, so that I could go shopping on the bus, sometimes only a few pilchards to be had. We did have a local village shop but, of course, everything was rationed. There was great excitement when some broken biscuits came in, and a few things "under the counter". Apart from the Valley regular buses we had a little bus called Farmers which rattled along. Mr F was an irascible old man who turned off anyone he did not like. It just did a country round. It was so small and narrow that, by the time you

Not the least of all that you will prize among the blessings of peace — will be your Kayser-Bondor stockings. Perfectly sheer . . . beautifully full-fashioned to fit immaculately . . . in an array of fashionable shades . . . *these* are the promise of Kayser-Bondor!

KAYSER-BONDOR

By 1945 how we longed for those 'perfectly sheer' new stockings that were 'among the blessings of peace'!

alighted, your coats were half off your back and it was a real struggle with shopping. He had a lovely Spanish wife who sometimes travelled with him, with a large comb in her hair. She kept him in order. I had to push Baby up Coombe Lane, gradient 1 in 6, to the local clinic. Going up was hard work but coming down was worse as I was not very muscular and in constant dread of the pram running away down the steep hill. The only way was to tack across the road, not much traffic but awful sharp bends.

'When the doodlebugs started to fall, we had to cover Baby's cot because of flying glass. We were within a mile of the extent of their range, so knew when we heard one that it would surely fall. One night, John had just got into bed (he had worked all day and all night and he fell into bed exhausted). A doodle came over and fell opposite the east window of the church, completely shattering it. The blast came up the valley and sucked down the ceiling in our back bedroom. Some friends of ours who had come for a respite from London bombing came into our front bedroom with piles of plaster on their heads and shoulders expecting to find the worst. We were quite safe, but spent all day (August Bank Holiday Monday) carrying baths of rubble down the stairs. Blast had some very strange effects. One evening in April at dusk, we had a shower of firebombs in a wood opposite. As it was April the young leaves were appearing and, lit from below, the effect was so beautiful, a lovely translucent green.'

Mary Simmons (Wheeler End) recalls the struggle her mother *Mrs Doreen Wright (Little Chalfont)* had to keep things going at home. 'My father was in the Auxiliary 603 Squadron and his partner was in the Army, so Mother was left to run the family business. She told me she went to the Ministry to get war work, repairing lorries. I remember her trying to get the till to balance at Little Chalfont. Dad was shot down in his Hurricane over France, so she was left to bring up my twin brother and myself. Times were hard and I remember the tennis court had been turned into a rabbit run. When the cage got to the other end, we knew "Peter Rabbit" was for the pot and we would have new gloves for the winter. The smell of burning chicken food still remains vivid in my memory. She made hankies out of flour bags (they were very rough) and lovely underwear from the silk parachutes.'

LOVE ONE ANOTHER

War brought strangers to even the smallest villages, including prisoners of war, both German and Italian, who often helped out on local farms. Even in such circumstances, friendships were made, but sometimes it was difficult to know exactly how to treat them. As a child, *Prudence Goodwin (Wingrave)* listened to her grandfather at Sunday school but 'could never understand the complexity of war. We were told to love one another on Sunday and the next day when all the prisoners of war gathered at the top of Nup End it was more than our life was worth to even look at them, leave alone speak. I always felt sorry for them in their brown serge outfits with a big patch on the back.'

A HUGE ADVENTURE

Many villages in rural Buckinghamshire welcomed evacuees, usually young children moved en masse from more dangerous areas. *Jean Brinded (Wingrave)* watched them arrive: 'We were all on the village green when the evacuees came in double decker buses. They were all scared as they didn't know where they were going to live. We had two small girls to live with us and they still keep in touch after all these years.'

Lisbeth Lloyd, with her sister *Cherry-Ann Evans (Wingrave)*, was herself an evacuee and remembers the experience from another perspective:

'My sister and I came to Wingrave under the Government scheme for evacuation, organised together with our London school. On Friday, 1st September 1939, in a group of 30 children, we eventually arrived, very tired, rather dishevelled, waiting in the school hall to be billeted.

'Fortunately, our mother had come with us, to be a teacher's help, which meant that she had to take the children to their new homes where they would be looked after by the kind people of Wingrave, who opened their houses and their arms to us all. We were billeted with a lovely newly married couple, Mr and Mrs Cliff Woodruff, or as we came to call them Aunty Ivy and Uncle Cliff. Life to my sister and I seemed like a huge adventure, as we explored and got to know Wingrave. My father worked up in London and stayed in the flat, but he soon wanted to be with us so my mother, after a few months, was able to get a tiny cottage in the village, and we lived in it until the war was over.

'Among the hundreds of memories we have, one stands out as truly amazing: the evening we went carol singing. It was Christmas Eve, and we were at the end of our tour around the village. We had arrived at the Manor House, where Dr Benej the Czech President was living in exile. We were never to disturb him, we knew this, but feeling very tired and hungry we did the forbidden thing and knocked on the door in the wall. To our utter amazement, it opened and we were ushered inside. The scene was absolutely magical, for there standing on the step, was Dr Benej himself with all his staff. We could glimpse the lit-up tree in the Great Hall and, as the snow gently began to fall, we sang our hearts out for them, all our carols, and ended up with a carol called *Rocking*, which was a Czech carol, but we did not know this.

'With tears streaming down their faces, our audience stood for a moment, in silence . . . then with thunderous applause, they cheered, hugged and kissed us, and I remember being picked up and swirled around the lawn by the cook! Inside were hot drinks and buns, and Dr Benej was very generous and put a lot of notes into our tin which, by the way, was labelled "Mrs Churchill's Aid to Russia".

'And so we stayed on in the village, delighting at its safeness, its seasons, we came from childhood to adult-hood. When we look back on our childhood, we think of it as a very special time of our lives . . . one which neither of us will ever forget.

'Here is a little poem I wrote of what may go through a little lad's mind as he gets on a train to be evacuated.

EVACUATION

The whistle blew
Say goodbye
To the world you knew,
Gas-mask at the ready,
Hey, go steady,
Don't forget to write.
Soon be there,
In safer places,
Fields to run in,

New play-mates to meet,
New life to greet,
Here we are ... Hello son.
Please God ... I want me Mum.'

SAVINGS AND SALVAGE

Civilians throughout the country threw themselves into the war effort with a will. Everyone was urged to collect salvage and support the troops, not to waste anything, to 'make do and mend', and 'dig for Victory' by turning every small patch of land over to fruit and vegetable production.

'We were very fortunate in Westbury during the war,' said *Ray Cook (Westbury and Shalstone).* 'Only one bomb was dropped nearby, on a tennis court in Finmere. It released all the pigs which were penned on it. We had First Aid classes which were well attended and most of the ladies knitted socks, gloves and balaclava helmets to send to the troops – how fortunate we were that none of our Westbury men were injured. About 30 evacuees were accommodated here and still correspond with the families who took them in and cared for them.'

Wingrave WI's notes, sent in by Mary Mountain and Betty Carter, for the war period are an indication of the time and hard work put in by Buckinghamshire women during those difficult years, which did not end in 1945!

Comforts for Forces	(knitting socks, scarves sweaters etc for those on active service)
Dec 1939	Receipts for gift stall to be used to buy 6 lbs khaki wool. Secretary to apply to Bucks HQ Comforts Fund.
Dec 1941	Member appointed wool distributor. Miss Rand has made 19 pairs of socks during the year.
Dec 1942	Total of knitted garments to date 335, including 26 for British POWs.
Dec 1943	160 garments in the last 2 years; Miss Rand – 83 pairs of socks, 1 pullover and 2 scarves.
Sep 1944	Knitting for relief in Europe; 2 lbs wool/Institute/month allocated.

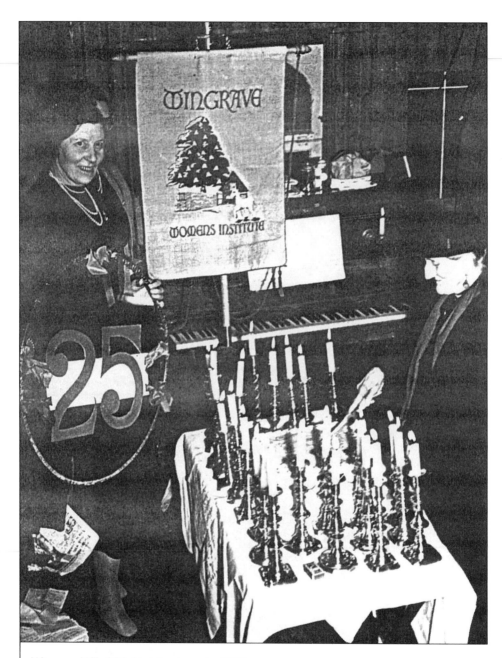

Wingrave WI's 25th birthday party in 1950,
a time to look to the future after the war years.
(Wingrave WI)

Dec 1944	67 garments for Europe; Miss Rand total now 100.
May 1946	Plaque from RAF in gratitude for knitting to be hung in Temperance Hall.

Stamp Collection (postage stamps were collected to raise money for the hospitals)

Dec 1939	12 tons GB stamps and 1 ton foreign realised £1,425.
Dec 1940	1,000,000 stamps to hospital.
Dec 1942	Stamp collection for Tindal Hospital.

Salvage and Gifts to Forces (paper, metal, wood, glass – everything had a salvage value that could raise money and help the war effort)

Dec 1941	982 lbs salvage collected to be sold to finance jam-making.
Nov 1942	Money from salvage to be sent to boys in Forces; postal order 7/6d each.
Nov 1943	Preservation Fund closed: two thirds to Troops Christmas Fund, one third to NFWI.
Dec 1943	Christmas gifts added to list – airmen and 4 airmen stationed in village (2 of these married village girls and staying); ATS and husbands of girls in Forces – 7/6d each.
Jan 1945	Christmas gifts sent to 66 members of Forces.
April 1945	Nurse added to list. Fund for Service men and women closed. Salvage collection taken over by District Council; treat to be given to children who collected.
Jan 1946	40 children/2 adults to pantomime in Amersham.

Whist (we could enjoy ourselves at the same time as raising money – regular drives were held; cards borrowed by other village organisations)

March 1942	A charge of 2s made for hire of cards "as they are getting dilapidated".
April 1943	Whist drive for Russia – £11.
Feb 1947	Whist drive for flood victims.

Meat pies (WIs were at the forefront of the government's scheme to ensure agricultural and manual workers got the food they needed during the working day)

June 1943	Agricultural and manual workers unable to get to British Restaurant or canteen may buy 2 pies a week – 40 names.
July 1943	Distribution began.
Feb 1946	Completely new pie list.
July 1947	£43 8s 0d returned to Institute from Government, being extra halfpenny on pies. Some opting out of pie purchase.
Sep 1947	6 extra requested.
Nov 1947	Delivery days changed. Allow 2 weeks to decide how many wish to continue. Rota for 2 weeks only then no more.
Oct 1948	Further £5 1s 11d returned from sale of pies.

Rose hips (an excellent source of Vitamin C, hips were gathered to be made nationally into syrup for children)

July 1943	Collection.
Feb 1945	11 tons 8 cwt from Oxon and Bucks.

Gifts from abroad (life on rations could be boring – parcels from abroad were always welcome)

Jan 1944	Tomato seeds from Canada.
Nov 1945	72 lbs cocoa to be distributed between men and women over 70.
Sep 1946	Parcel from Australia "shared by 7 lucky winners".

An advertisement from 1946 – it was still important to make the most of home-grown fruit and veg.

Miscellaneous

Dec 1941	Demonstration of net camouflage at meeting.
Aug 1942	No canning this year as sugar and cans not to hand.
July 1943	Red Cross Book Campaign. Try to collect 150 books for Red Cross and St John's Library.
April 1945	82 members, 32 at meeting (some members only joined to be able to go to the prestigious Party).
April 1946	Royal Bucks Hospital asked members to organise egg collection for their patients.
Dec 1946	Auditor given 50 cigarettes "for his kind help".
June 1947	Old folks (60) to tea and entertainment.
Dec 1947	Cigarettes to auditor and to Mr Taylor for supplying milk for meeting. Decided to put seat on Green. Difficulty in supply; obtained with permit. To put on brass plaque.
May 1948	3 members to embroider panel for wedding present for Princess Elizabeth.

CHAPTER TWO
HALL BARN —
A GREAT HOUSE 1939-1969

H all Barn is one of Beaconsfield's treasures, built by Edmund Waller in the 17th century.

Mrs L. Whitehead (Beaconsfield Old Town) describes the ups and downs of life in the house through the war and in the years after, at a time when many great houses were having to adjust to new times and new pressures.

'It was barely a week after the outbreak of World War II that the first pantechnicon arrived outside the front door to deliver pictures and furniture from the Wallace Collection for safe keeping from enemy action. The Long Parlour and the Ballroom became a treasure trove of the finest antiques in the country. The Ballroom being 30 feet square with highly polished parquet flooring, housed most of the pictures in packing cases. The Long Parlour, 78 feet long by 20 feet wide, was covered by druggets to protect the floor before moving in the heavy furniture. In charge of the whole operation was James Mann, the Curator and a band of 16 of the commissionaires from the museum in London. All the staff remained billeted in the house and stables for the duration. An amusing incident occurred as a result of so many strangers around the place when my mother met a strange couple coming upstairs so rather naturally asked who they were and what they were doing, only to be told quite calmly, "We live here". It was the Curator and his wife who lived in rooms on the very top floor.

'On fine summer days we had the immense pleasure of looking at beautiful pieces of furniture and pictures brought out for polishing and checking and inspecting on the lawn outside the house. The other "evacuees" were the armour from the Tower of London including the block and the axe. The latter gave my brother and me, when we were home on leave, the excitement of ghost hunting but regretfully neither of us ever saw a headless figure wandering around.

'In 1941, the Government decided that more treasures should be evacuated from London and we took delivery of the painted ceiling from the Banqueting Hall at Whitehall, transported on the largest lorry ever seen in those days. It had to be moved in through the french windows off the terrace as that was the

The ballroom stacked with packing cases,
mostly containing pictures from the Wallace Collection.
(Mrs L. Whitehead – Beaconsfield Old Town)

only entrance door high enough. It then occupied the whole of the Long Gallery leaving only the front and back doors usable by the owners.

'During the whole of the war period 1939–1945, the house was also used as the Central Hospitals Supply Service Depot with the Library, another of the 30 foot square rooms, stacked high with boxes of many-tailed bandages, surgical dressings and clothing for bomb casualties as well as wounded service personnel. This room had to have its 27 foot square carpet removed by the

Checking stores for the
Central Hospital Supply Service.
(Mrs L. Whitehead – Beaconsfield)

The children of the house helping out — the small boy is Hugh Hudson, director of the film Chariots of Fire. (Mrs L. Whitehead — Beaconsfield)

Wallace Collection staff who took it out onto the lawn to shake and roll up for the duration. The CHSS operation was run by my mother as head of the British Red Cross in Buckinghamshire, and a noble band of volunteers. Until I was old enough to join the ATS at 18, my job was to deliver the supplies to hospitals around the country which gained me the privilege of driving a car with a Special Driving Licence to carry out the work without passing a driving test – to this day I have still not passed a test as I was issued with an army licence on demobilisation which the authorities accepted for the issue of a civilian licence.

'The only large room remaining free for use by the family was the dining room which became a sitting/dining room. One more room on the ground floor became an office with a secretary acting for CHSS and additionally my mother's work with the Red Cross, the Girl Guides and her duties as Branch President of the WI from 1935–1946. The latter kept her busy with the annual WI pantomime. There was a queue for the three performances and it was always a complete sell out.

'It was a very full, busy and happy home for three members of the family whenever they came home on leave from the army, bearing the popular ration cards and petrol coupons, but also managing to house two army officers working on secret duties at Wilton Park. Running the house was difficult at times for those staff remaining after the Lord of the Manor had gone to fight in France the first week of September 1939, taking the chef as his Headquarters cook, the chauffeur as his driver, and the butler as his batman. The kitchen maid lived in the house but worked at a munitions factory in Beaconsfield. One of my clear memories is of Walter Kirby arriving at the back door with the horse and cart to collect the swill from the house for the one pig each household was allowed to keep. The head groom Fred Wooler was relegated, to his disgust, to milking the one cow since all the horses had been either "called up" or turned out to grass.

'Many fund raising events took place in the grounds, such as the 1943 Wings for Victory campaign.

'After the war the house returned to its proper role as a place for weekend parties, balls and more activities arising from the organisations with which the Lady of the Manor was connected, culminating in the International Camp for 1,500 Girl Guides in 1951.

Above and below – at the Wings for Victory fund raising fete.
(Mrs L. Whitehead – Beaconsfield Old Town)

'The death in 1963 of the 4th Lord Burnham changed everything. The house sadly became empty without sufficient finances, due to death duties, to run an establishment with 28 bedrooms.

'In a determined effort to avoid having to sell the property, various avenues were explored. One of these resulted in it being let to the younger brother of the Sheik of Abu Dhabi, called Sheik Zaid who had been obliged to leave his country to avoid being accused of murder during an uprising against the reigning ruler. The harem consisting of four wives, their children and attendant eunuch occupied one wing of the house which was cut off by a locked door with only the Sheik and the eunuch holding a key. The existing house staff were retired to cottages on the estate and the Ottoman Bank engaged replacements. The cook was Turkish and is recorded as having chased some of the staff round the house with a hatchet. The youngest wife

The house disguised for a film as the Australian Embassy in Belgravia Square, London, 1968. (Mrs L. Whitehead – Beaconsfield Old Town)

was 14 years old and the senior wife remained in Abu Dhabi although her son and heir came to Hall Barn. Aged ten, the only thing he wanted was a bicycle, which was obtained from Hamleys, and he could be seen pedalling furiously up and down the drive with two fully armed Arab guards in flowing robes running beside him. Dramas occurred at regular intervals but, as far as the family was concerned, the only serious one was when a black Labrador decided to return to his old home drawn by the smell of cooking and ended up in the harem amongst screaming women because dogs in their country were unclean. Dinner on the first night resulted in the carpet being covered in discarded chicken bones. The next day the Ottoman Bank, fearful of the damages bill, brought in a large plastic sheet to cover the entire floor. This period lasted two years until Sheik Zaid was able to return to rule his country after the revolution.

'From 1965 to 1969 the house stood empty, only being used from time to time as a film set, the rent helping to keep the property in some sort of repair. The best known full length film was the drama centred on the Australian Ambassador to London accused of a murder. It starred Christopher Plummer and was called *Nobody Runs For Ever*. The gravel forecourt was transformed to represent the embassy in London with loads of laurels being brought down.

'After long discussions within the family and the employment of professionals, it was decided to demolish two thirds of the house, including all the big reception rooms, and restore it to the original of 1680 known as "Edmund Waller's town box". This transformation was only achieved by the sale of all the treasures in the house that would no longer have a place, the proceeds to be used for the rebuilding work. In the summer of 1969, the demolition contractors started work and Hall Barn as a great house became only a memory in the mind of the family still living.'

CHAPTER THREE
HOME AND VILLAGE LIFE

'No running water or bathrooms, not for most of us.'
(Pamela Allen – Winslow)

'One large coal fire in the black-leaded grate, always burning, with a black kettle on the side for instant hot water at any time,' was at the heart of home life for *Pamela Allen (Winslow)* in the 1940s. 'A brick in the oven to get hot for bedtime which was wrapped in an old pillow case to keep you warm, among the sticks which were drying off. We would go over the fields to get wood for the fire. When we got home we would boil the kettle for tea with the wood we had brought back. We called it a "blizzie". We toasted crumpets for tea on a long fork by the fire. It would burn your hand and you would drop the toast or crumpet in the ashes. You picked it up, blew on it and put butter on it. Couldn't waste anything.'

Keeping warm could be difficult in those days before central heating and double glazing. 'Winters were cold at home,' for *Pat Heath (Downley Village Evening)*, 'the only fire was in the living room except for the coal-burning boiler in the kitchen. Frost patterns formed inside the windows, and there were frozen flannels in the bathroom and very cold lino on the floor.'

And the cold felt even worse when you had to go outside for every call of nature! It was dark out there too, as *Avril Hartin (Downley Village Evening)* recalled. 'Mum, Dad and I lived with my grandparents in a very old lodge house, with no electricity, no bathroom, and an outside toilet down the yard. This had quite an effect. Being scared of the dark has played a part in my life due to all the visits down the yard.'

'The loo paper was the *News of the World* or something similar,' said *Pamela Allen (Winslow)*, 'cut into squares and threaded through on a piece of string and hooked on a nail at the back of the loo door. When it was dark and you wanted to go, you went down the yard with a candle which would blow out in the wind. If you got there with the candle still alight it was quite ghostly and very cold, always frozen in winter. Four bricks were kept out of the top to let in fresh air – no windows.'

There were other hazards. 'In the 1940s when I was 15 years old we still had a bucket lavatory,' recalled *Mrs B. Woodward (Wheeler End)*. 'We also rented some fields, one of which we opened up to campers, coming mostly from London. My brother, younger than me, picked a bunch of stinging nettles, opened the door at the back of the loo and pushed them in. Poor Emily who was on the loo at the time swore we had woodworm in the seat. You can bet we never owned up.'

Of course, cesspits needed regular emptying. *Carole Bowler (Hazlemere)* says that 'occasionally Dirty Dennis would be emptying somebody's cesspit along the road and the boys would enjoy jumping back and forth over the pipe shouting "rude" words such as "stink" or "pong" – we girls would hold our noses and hustle away. It was not until 1961 that main drainage came to the Hughenden Valley and we were invaded by cheeky but harmless Irish workmen laying the pipes.'

WASHDAY

With no running water laid on, washday was still as hard and unpleasant a day for women in the Forties as it had been for generations, as *Pamela Allen (Winslow)* explains:

'Monday was always cold meat and home-made chutney or pickled onions for dinner, with fried up vegetables in "bubble and squeak" – very nice. But Monday was also washday, when the kitchen was changed from a warm cosy place to a hovel in no time at all.

'A large tin bath on the table to do the coloured washing in, with a big bar of green soap for collar and cuffs, rubbed on to get them clean. The whites went into the copper with the "blue bag" to whiten them. The copper had to be filled with water and a fire lit under it with sticks and cardboard boxes to get it to boiling point.

'When the washing was finished it would go on the line, pegged on with dolly pegs which we bought from a gipsy at the door. If you had a mangle you

By the late 1950s, washing machines were making life easier and Persil had become everyone's favourite washing powder.

Ewbank

Limited deliveries
will commence in
a few weeks' time.

THE WORLD'S BEST CARPET SWEEPER

In 1946 we were being assured that we would be getting back to normal – soon!

would put the clothes through – neatly, or they would jam the works. If you did it level, you didn't have to do so much ironing. It all then had to be aired by the fire. You can quite see why people only changed their clothes once a week.

'The suds left from the washing couldn't be wasted as all water had to be carried from a pump in the back garden or local alleyway. We would use it to wash down the kitchen and toilet floors.

'Tuesday you would do the ironing. You heated up a flat iron on the fire – to see if it was hot you spat on it and if it sizzled, it was. You would have a "holder" – made from an old towel was best – to pick it up with or you would burn your hand.'

THE SILVER REFLECTS:

Besides the shining picture of the room that I adorn you can see in me, as in a magic mirror, a woman's loving care, her pride in her home, and her gratitude to Silvo for the gleaming beauty which it gives, so carefully, to her treasured silver things. **SILVO**

Back to the home, ladies, after your wartime efforts and polish that silver – an advertisement from 1946.

PRIDE AND JOY

In *Carole Bowler's (Hazlemere Evening)* childhood kitchen, the old and the new were meeting – still cold, still basic, but her mother had some new appliances to be proud of:

'A morning in January 1950. Time to drag all my clothes into bed to warm them up – a woollen vest, the loathed liberty bodice with redundant rubber buttons, two pairs of sturdy Chilprufe knickers complete with handkerchief pockets and thick football-type socks. Speed was vital whilst getting dressed in order to keep warm – as I pulled back the unlined floral curtains once again there were the exquisite patterns of ice covering the inside of the window pane. No point in visiting the bathroom. The bath and basin had been frozen since Boxing Day.

'I slid down the bannisters to the quarry-tiled kitchen warmed by the solid fuel Rayburn range. My mother's pride and joy, a new Thor washing machine was at the opposite end of the room and next to a small Belling electric cooker with two solid hot plates.'

Modern kitchen appliances were still only a dream for most women. But *Muriel King (Taplow & Hitcham)* recalls her first refrigerator.

'We had been married for five years when we moved into a brand new house in 1947. Previously we had lived in my parents' house (circa 1900) which had a larder with a marble shelf to keep food cool and fresh.

'As a surprise my husband had bought a fridge – a large cupboard-like object which took up a lot of room in my small kitchen. Powered by gas, it had a

1955, and how happy she looks.

Even Debonair magic won't dry babies!

but it will dry everything else you wash

. . . ready for ironing or airing in a matter of minutes.

Nappies, yes . . . cottons, linens, woollens, non-iron fabrics, blankets . . . *everything washable* can be safely left to the fast drying magic of the Creda Debonair. Takes the sting out of wash-day—gives the *certainty* of ironing four minutes after washing . . . any hour of the day . . . any day of the year . . . in any weather.

The Debonair is outstanding: the first all-British spindryer—and unquestionably the best for a multitude of reasons. Better made, better finished and above all, safest and most efficient.

Creda Debonair

Britain's first and finest spindryer

9 Purchasers out of 10 have chosen Creda Debonair.

There must be good reasons.

Debonair Efficiency—faster spinning speed of the Debonair gives added moisture extraction making clothes really ready for immediate ironing.

Debonair Drying Times—from 4 minutes for blankets to 4 seconds for non-iron fabrics.

Debonair Safety—it's positive! Lock the lid it starts, unlock the lid it automatically stops.

Debonair Mobility—wheels smoothly—yet patented mounting ensures steadiness during spinning.

Debonair Protection—no heat to felt or shrink woollens. Gentle action safe for flimsies, buttons, fasteners.

Debonair Capacity — family wash, even a full size double blanket, yet stows away neatly.

Debonair Economy—100 loads for 1d. worth of electricity.

Debonair Quality—built to incomparable Creda standards.

Debonair Value—Creda quality, efficiency, safety for £32. 0. 9. (P.T. paid) or easy terms.

You WILL buy a spindryer—compare Creda "plus" features before deciding —nothing less will satisfy you.

SIMPLEX ELECTRIC CO. LTD., *London Showrooms:* Creda House, Binney Street, London, W.1. A COMPANY

If you couldn't afford a washing machine, the next best thing was a spin drier.

grille top and bottom of the door and it gave off fumes, so I had to keep a window open all the time. Opening the back door, the gas frequently blew out and I had to get down on my hands and knees to relight it.

'Good, I thought, no more milk going sour and not having to cover meat will be a distinct advantage. Perhaps I could make the children ice cream? Turning to my one and only cookery book, I found instructions on how to use a vacuum freezer and making ice cream without freezing but it said nothing about a refrigerator. But I thought "Economical Ice Cream" sounded good, though with rationing still on I had no sugar to spare or a vanilla pod, but I had saved a sheet of gelatine and I had some dried milk. What turned out looked like a pale yellow custard, and 24 hours later after resting in the fridge we attacked this solid block. That was the first and last time I made ice cream, even though the fridge lasted us well for ten years.'

Janet Cross (Horn Hill) came to Buckinghamshire in 1946. 'I had a fridge, but little else in the way of help with the chores. Soon we acquired a washing machine, which was a great joy, but not until a lot later did I have a freezer, dishwasher and tumble drier.'

But times were changing very rapidly now, as *Lindsey Haubner (Coleshill)* notes. 'In 1950 and 1951, the biggest change to our village was the new housing estate at Hill Meadow. Local builder, Maurice Weller also built several new, detached houses in the village. Everyone not only wanted plumbing and bathrooms now but also luxuries like washing machines and refrigerators and, by the Sixties, televisions and record players were becoming commonplace as well as the new central heating.'

COST OF LIVING

Doris Shelley (Penn & Tylers Green Evening) moved to her new house on the Deer Park estate in Tylers Green in January 1959.

'The price of a new three-bedroomed semi-detached house on the estate was just under £3,000! I see from my 1966 diary that I was given a housekeeping allowance of £35 which had to last me a month, and this was raised to £43 a month by 1969! There were six of us in the family, and we had a small car. I made my own clothes and most of my children's, and I note that in 1966 I had to buy my 15 year old son a coat, trousers and a pair of shoes, costing me £7,

£3 and £2 respectively. In 1969 (still pre-decimal currency) the milk bill for my family was £1 10s 7d, which works out at 21 pints a week at 1s 5d (about 7p) a pint. Now I pay my milkman the equivalent of 8 shillings a bottle for my daily pint of milk! My copy of the Radio Times was just 6d then (2p). It's 79 pence now.

'I remember paying 10d (4p) to get to High Wycombe from Tylers Green by bus in early 1959, with weekly visits to Beaconsfield on a regular bus service which, alas, no longer runs since it appears to be no longer viable. And my train fare to London used to be just over £1!'

VILLAGE LIFE

'Maybe we tend to take for granted improvements to our village environment that have taken place over the years,' suggested *Rosemary Saunders (Winchmore Hill)*. But she goes on:

'My husband and I, with our young son, came to live in Winchmore Hill in the 1950s. The village then was not quite the "highly desirable area" described today in estate agents' advertisements. It was still pretty rural, with two old pubs, no newly built houses, only two street lights (one at the top and one at the bottom of the village), and a very rough and overgrown village common, not groomed several times a year as it is now.

'At that time in the Fifties, however, we did have some advantages of note. There was a good and regular bus service (every 20 or 30 minutes mornings and evenings if I remember correctly, fare into Amersham 6d). We had our own "lengthman" who swept the roads and kept the edges tidy, and our own policeman – both of them shared with neighbouring villages. We had a thriving corner shop-cum-post office, an excellent butcher licensed to sell game, and a visiting baker (now all we have is a small post office, open five mornings a week only). Whenever there was frost or snow our roads were regularly salted and sanded, so early in the day that my husband, leaving for work most days soon after 7 am, hardly ever saw the sanding vehicles.

'Perhaps most noteworthy of all, we had little or no crime in those days. Indeed, whenever my husband and I went out we never used to lock our house, and the postman, when he called twice daily, would open our back door, leave whatever letters or parcels he had for us in the kitchen and at the

Above and below – Great Missenden in the 1950s, almost car-free.
(Jeanne Keen and Margaret Couling – Gt Missenden Evening)

same time collect any we had left him for posting. Truly, not everything of the present day constitutes progress!'

Many would echo that sentiment. In the 1940s, *Jean Brinded (Wingrave)* says, 'everyone knew everyone else and we would all help each other. Nowadays you don't even know your neighbours.'

Lindsey Haubner (Coleshill) agreed. 'Because everyone knew everybody else, it was always known if someone was seriously ill. Until the war, if a man died, the church bell rang three times. For a lady it was twice and a child once. There was far more respect and grown-ups were always referred to as Mrs or Mr by children. There was no malicious vandalism but a fair bit of cheeky mischief. If a child went a little too far then a word was had to his or her parents and a stern telling off would usually sort out the problem.'

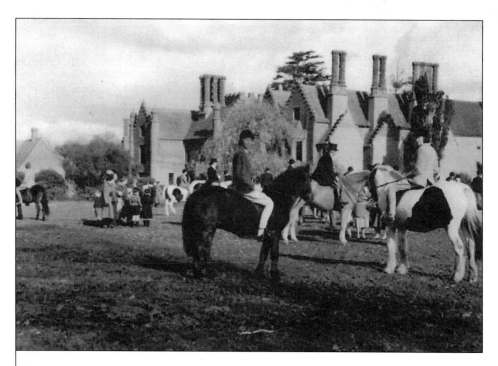

A Meet at Chenies
manor house in the 1950s.
(Janet Cross – Horn Hill)

BITTERLY COLD

Good neighbourliness was often brought out by hard times – and the severe winters of 1947 and 1962/3 were certainly that, as *Betty Hiscock (Water Eaton)* recalled.

'Boxing Day 1962, it was bitterly cold, my in-laws were staying with us, other relations had arrived by car.

'Once during the evening someone remarked, "The car is covered in snow". It passed unnoticed – we were enjoying our festive celebrations, games competitions, eating far too much and, in those days, the alcohol flowed freely.

'At 2.30 am, our visitors decided that it was time to depart. Before they could

*The winter of 1947 was one of the worst we have endured,
cutting off villages and stopping life in its tracks – and
coal was still on ration.
(Margaret Haradine – Hanslope)*

reach the car, it was all hands on deck to shovel away the snow. My father-in-law observed, "I didn't realise it was so deep". By this time the moon was shining and it was freezing hard.

'Just after 3 am, the car at last slid down the road, the driver unable to steer a straight course.

'That night was the beginning of weeks of ice and snow. The car that would not start was to be a minor incident, and there emerged a great spirit of neighbourliness.

'Oh, that we had not used so much coal over Christmas. Early January saw our supply dwindling and the coalman just did not appear. To the rescue came my next-door neighbour (he always came up trumps). His firm's lorry was sent to a nearby village coal yard and stocks of precious fuel were deposited in our barn. Breathe again.

'Three days later, no water. Frantic efforts all in vain. The outside supply pipe to the house had frozen. Luckily my neighbour's was still unfrozen. Never realised just how much water one used. In snow and ice, kettles and saucepans of water were fetched from next door. Spill a little outside and it froze. Ingenuity on my neighbour's part: a large milk churn arrived and was placed in the kitchen. A hose pipe through next door's window, and the churn was regularly filled. This provided water for washing and flushing loos. I can still feel the chill when the back door was opened.

'Another friend who still had her water supply asked, "Would you like a bath?" I jumped at the idea, the water in the churn would not run to baths. As I emerged from her cold bathroom, she said, "Sorry, it was chilly in there, none of us have braved it for a week". Rushed home to my coal fire.

'One very still frosty early evening, with a mantle of snow outside – it was so quiet. Then there was a terrific bang in the house which shattered the silence. Husband at work, so rushed round next door frightened to death. What catastrophe had befallen? Investigated: a bottle of lemonade had frozen, then exploded.

'Those were the good old days, when adversity brought out the spirit of good neighbours, even if I was teased for weeks about the lemonade.'

HOW AYLESBURY HAS GROWN

Margaret Mortham (Broughton Pastures) came to live in Aylesbury in 1957, and her story shows the pace of change in just a decade or so after the war.

'In 1957 a new three bedroom semi-detached house on the outskirts of Aylesbury was £2,350. After working for the NHS for six years, when my weekly wage was £1 10s, I had managed to save £100. My fiancé, as he was then, had about £500. The deposit for the house was £235, so we had a week's honeymoon in Minehead, Devon, and furnished our first home with the remainder. The only new item we had was a cooker; we had a second-hand bed with orange boxes for bedside tables. Thick dried mud covered every floor inside the house, but to start with we had to sit on the bare floor to eat as we had no chairs and no carpets. We thought we were lucky to have a house of our own and did not worry about "luxuries".

'We were the last occupants at the far end of a building site and the nearest shops, a butcher and post office-cum-general store, were 15 minutes walk away. No bus came near us and we had no car. The quickest way to the Aylesbury shops was along a muddy lane and over the canal, about a 20 minute walk or if it was too wet we had to go along the road which was a 40 minute walk. There was a grocery shop in the High Street which sold things cheaper than elsewhere, sugar was weighed out in the shop in large thick blue paper bags.

'Our garden backed onto a farmer's field and was just as the builders had left it, with lumps of cement tipped from the mixers, bricks, scaffold poles and boards. All had to be removed before we could make a lawn. In the middle of one night we were awoken to find almost a complete herd of cows had broken through the hedge and trampled along everyone's newly growing grass and were madly calling to their few pals left in the field. Some earlier residents had their vegetable gardens stripped bare while we had hoof marks on our lawn for years to remind us of our unwelcome visitors.

'While walking down the muddy lane towards the town centre we passed what had been a wartime temporary housing estate. The buildings had gone but the gardens remained so we, and many other neighbours, rescued some of the plants to help start our gardens. I still have large juicy blackberries each autumn.

'There were no telephones on the estate but we needed one for emergency use: at that time there was a year's waiting list. As my husband was on call for the local hospital, they applied for one to be fitted urgently. Until this was done, they sent a taxi to collect him each time he was needed in a hurry. One night the driver muddled the house number and knocked on the door of no 39 instead of 89. We never heard what they thought of being woken at 3 am by a taxi wanting to whisk them off to hospital immediately! The journey to the hospital was over three miles by road but a short cut for walking was across two fields and under the railway line. At first my husband walked this way to work until he found himself in the middle of a large field containing a herd of cows, including a bull! After that he carried his bicycle across one field and then cycled along the road, this cut over a mile off the journey.

'We had street lights along our road but they were switched off before midnight so it was very dark and eerie, being at the far end of the building site. Before long, the road opposite our house was built on and also the nearby muddy lane which, I believe, had been the original route from Aylesbury to London (I imagine horses and carriages travelling along there). We began to feel not quite so isolated. It was also possible to walk into the town centre along the previously muddy lane and arrive with clean shoes.

'Aylesbury had a choice of two cinemas with a change of films each week, possibly twice a week. The Borough Assembly Hall in Market Square put on very good amateur shows; this is where Ronnie Barker began his stage career. There was a flourishing cattle market and a twice weekly market where other goods could be bought. For what was described as a "sleepy market town", we had a good variety of shops and, before long, a superb new Woolworths was opened, where the present county library is. This was hailed as the biggest and best in Europe, on three floors with escalators instead of stairs! It was the beginning of the centre of Aylesbury being "up-dated". Many lovely little roads and shops were demolished and what we now know as Friars Square was built (although this has since been revamped again). Some of the shops were temporarily housed in a row of garages during rebuilding work.

'In 1961, the routine was for all babies to be born at home, probably because the hospital was too small for the rapidly expanding town. As we were both NHS staff, I was allowed to have my first baby in hospital. The consultant said, "It would be a poor thing if we could not look after our own staff". I was in a room with three other NHS staff which was very nice and friendly but I was not allowed home for ten days even though there had been no problems with either myself or the baby. I was really exhausted when I was discharged and had to cope with a home and a new baby. Looking back, I realised it was because there had been no reason to get out of bed in hospital, we just sat and chatted all the time.

'By 1964, when I had my next baby, I stayed at home so that I was not away from our daughter for any length of time. I was out of bed from the first day, wandering around the house and garden, doing a few chores and did not feel anywhere near so exhausted as I had previously.

'When we bought our house we were told the farm at the bottom of the garden was earmarked for another housing estate, but we were happy that building was not due to commence for about 20 years. Ten years later, a large estate was there including schools, shops, pubs and churches, also a bus service. These amenities were and still are very useful but, at the time, we felt rather cheated as we had enjoyed living virtually in the country. Aylesbury was designated as a "London overspill town", and in these few years it grew enormously, with a London accent being the one most often heard, as it still is.

'Our daughter was over five years old before she could start school, which was more than a mile walk from home. A nearer school was built on the new estate so she transferred there after a couple of years. Our son started at this school, but not until he was nearly five years six months old. By the time he was old enough for the next move, yet another school was opened even closer to home so he transferred there. From a single school in this area there were now six, a definite sign of how this side of Aylesbury has grown.'

OH NO, NOT ANOTHER ONE!

Home birth, or hospital maternity care? The 'fashion' moved away from home births after the war, but *Ann Colsell (West Wycombe)* had a very special reason for going into hospital in 1966 – three very special reasons, in fact.

'On 17th December 1963 my first baby Timothy was born at home in Chorley Road, West Wycombe. The nurse came down from Naphill in her little black car and I can still remember the comfort and reassurance she brought with

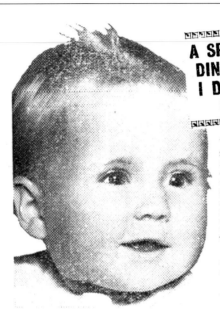
'Happiness all round' promised in an ad from 1946.

her. She took charge, sending my husband David downstairs to boil water and be kept company by his mother who had been called to help.

'Meanwhile, upstairs, nurse sorted me out, examined me, pronounced me doing well, brought out the gas and air and told me how to use it. That was wonderful, made me feel all floaty and unreal, and it didn't seem to take long before I was told to "push". I tried for a bit but when I found it just too hard nurse eased out the head. "Oh dear", she said, "hold fire a bit, the cord's round its neck. I'll have to cut it". I couldn't see what she did, but with her next instruction, "Right, now!" out popped the baby, a boy. He was a very funny colour, sort of blue, but nothing daunted, nurse gave him her instructions: "Come on, breathe!", she ordered, holding him upside down by his feet and slapping his back. And he did.

'She weighed him and found he was 7lb 15$^1/_2$oz. "Oh, we'll call that 8lb", she said.

'As she settled the baby and tidied me up, she said, "The next one will be easy, you'll see".

'The "next one", two years and four months later, turned out to be triplets. Diane, Paula and Robin were born in The Shrubbery, the maternity unit off Amersham Hill. Once again, I had excellent care. As I was so large at five months of pregnancy, I was sent for an x-ray and had to balance on this large bump on the x-ray table. I was asked to wait for the result and, when called

The Colsell family in 1969 – Robin, Diane, Paula and Timothy. (Ann Colsell – West Wycombe)

back to the consulting room, I will always remember Mr Butcher's words. "Come and sit down, I've something to show you. We've got three on here". He held up the x-ray plate and showed me three white blobs, which he said were heads, and three spines. One baby was across the top and, below it, one with head up and one head down.

'Mr Butcher was very kind and reassuring and told me they would have me in The Shrubbery at seven months for a rest.

'I went to tell David and Tim who had been waiting in the car and we sat there feeling as if we had been hit by a bomb blast.

'Anyway, I duly went into The Shrubbery and was given a room on my own, so that I could rest they said. We had a dining room, so I did meet other mothers and chat about babies – what else.

'Having nothing much to do, I concentrated on my breathing exercises for natural childbirth, using the small early contractions to practise on. Three weeks later, when I went into labour I found I could do it, and it worked, and I didn't need painkillers. Just as well, because I wasn't offered any until the very end when they brought out the gas and air. The babies were all born naturally between 6.30 pm and 7 pm and, when David came in at visiting time, he had a family of four.

'The people at The Shrubbery were wonderful, most of the staff seemed to be in at the birth and the babies were "theirs".

'Matron saw the *Cow and Gate* rep. who arranged for us to have free baby milk and all they wanted were a few photographs from time to time. This was a very real financial help.

'Matron asked if we would like to take all the babies home at once or one at a time. We opted for one at a time. Tim was overjoyed with his first little sister; thought his brother was all right; but when we went to fetch Paula, he said, "Oh no, not another one".

'That was our complete family. Matron had warned me to "shut-up shop" in case the next one was quads.'

CHAPTER FOUR
FOOD AND SHOPPING

'... tasty bread from the baker and the aroma of baking bread meeting you
as you opened the bakehouse door, and it was worth a smack on
the hand to nibble at the unwrapped loaf on my way home ...'

(Prudence Goodwin – Wingrave)

'In the 1940s,' recalled one lady from *Wingrave*, 'a regular visit to the village shop on a Saturday morning required not only a shopping list and money but a much needed ration book. Coupons made sure that each person had a weekly ration of butter and sugar. Then there was an allocation of points which could be spent on other products according to choice. These points could be used over a period of a month, so it was best to take it carefully for the first week or two and then at the end of the month there would be enough left for a treat. Tins of fruit were a luxury and we saved our points for those, I remember.

'Thinking about this now, what a nightmare it must have been for village shopkeepers. In addition to ordering their stock and counting their money, they had these flimsy pieces of paper to sort and count.

'Our village baker, whose face was always covered in flour and his hands with dough, never did cope with the bread units – BUs, as they came to be called. He used to raise his arms in despair as pieces of paper fluttered to the floor. He was so busy making and baking bread for the village folk that it was often twelve o'clock at night when he was riding round the village on his tricycle, with a large box attached to the front, delivering his loaves.

'Looking back, one realises how well everyone coped on both sides of the

counter. There was an air of grateful acceptance and appreciation of what one had got rather than grumbles and despair as to what could no longer be bought, with or without coupons or points.'

Janet Cross (Horn Hill) also remembers rationing. 'Food rationing continued for several years after we moved to Chalfont St Peter, but the children got used to at least one cheese based meal a week. Milk was difficult, as my three loved it. But there was milk powder which you whisked into water, which made a reasonable custard and other milk puddings. As regards sweets – they all liked Mars bars, and I cut them into equal slices, so that it was "fair". I didn't keep hens, but had a standing order with someone who did. I made great use of syrup for sweetening stewed fruit and spreading on bread. This was available on the "points" system. As we had a good-sized garden, we grew a lot of our own fruit and vegetables.'

Rationing in fact went on long after the war was over. Bread was rationed

Any hints on varying the monotony of rationing were welcome.

from 1946 to 1948, tea from 1940 to 1952, sweets from 1942 to 1953, jam from 1941 to 1948. Eggs came off ration in 1953, and sugar, while butter, cheese margarine and cooking fats followed the next year. Meat was the last – off ration in June 1954!

TREMENDOUS CHANGES

Barbara Richer (Princes Risborough Evening) worked for 50 years until her retirement in a local butcher's shop in Princes Risborough. 'As you can guess, tremendous changes have occurred from way back in 1945.

'Our display window was a huge marble slab, assisted by an inch and a half gap at the bottom of the shop window to help keep things cool.

'The days of rationing were difficult indeed. The shop owner was also a farmer and rabbits killed on the farm were a great attraction, causing many queues the days they arrived. When the local grocer had a few bananas it was almost a stampede.

'Throughout the war and until 1972, weekly deliveries were made to outlying villages. Their order was presented to the customer unwrapped, just in a wicker basket. Raw meat, corned beef rations, offal, bones etc, all just laid in the basket.

'Within the shop it was wooden counters and benches, which had to be scrubbed with very hot water and soda and plenty of elbow grease. No running water from the tap, just a copper in the corner. At the time that was very modern.

'The good old days? Not arf!'

SELF RELIANT

People were much more self reliant in the Forties and Fifties, as they had to be with few refrigerators and only limited supplies in the shops.

'We had a meat safe on the wall to keep the flies off and the meat cool,' said *Pat Heath (Downley Village Evening)*, 'and milk was kept in a bucket of cold water in the summer. My parents had a large garden and we had most of the vegetables you could grow then and several apple and plum trees, and soft fruit. During the autumn the pantry was stocked with jars of all this produce from the garden, bottled fruits mostly and blackberries for fruit pies, and alongside jars of jam. Fruits do not seem to taste like they used to – Victoria plums, for one!'

Most people bought their provisions at their local shop – no supermarkets then to walk around and take your pick. 'We took our lists and she would fetch the items for us, add it up in her head and we paid in cash – no plastic or cheques for us locals.

'We would pay 2s 6d a week in the Co-op club and when you got £5 you could go to Bletchley on the steam train to spend it – quite an event. The shop there had lots of departments and this was the nearest to a shopping centre we had then. You could buy a coat, shoes, skirt and jumper for about £5 then. And you got a "divi", a slip of paper with a number on it – everyone who went to the Co-op had one. Ours was 2219!

'Food shopping was basic then. Everyone made their own cakes and biscuits. Beef stew and dumplings, or meat pie, or roast beef on Sunday if you could afford it, with Yorkshire pudding, and rice pudding for afters. Spotted dick with custard. Bacon and onion clanger was also a good stand-by on a winter's day, with leeks and mash. The meal we called dinner was at 12 noon.'

HOME DELIVERY

People relied on the home delivery service that tradesmen offered, as *Jill Garland (Wingrave)* could confirm.

'My first husband, Fred Timms, was the village butcher. Because public transport was not very good, anyone wanting to get to London early in the day would have a lift to Aylesbury station on Monday morning when Fred drove in to collect his father at about 5.30 am. This was for their trip to Watford chilled-meat market to buy New Zealand lambs, etc, and he was usually back for his breakfast by 8 am. Several brides-to-be and their mothers and bridesmaids used this lift when going to London to buy their dresses.

'Villagers very rarely locked their back doors in those days and when we delivered the meat, the money and next week's order was often left on the table with a plate to put the meat on. We would either put the meat in the pantry or fridge. Sometimes we would be asked something like, "Are you going near my sister's house in Aston Abbots, would you drop this parcel in for me?" I think most delivery people were very helpful then. One lady who was feeding her newborn baby called out to my husband when he delivered the meat, "Quick, butcher, come up here, my baby cannot breathe". Fred had no first-aid knowledge, but he picked up the baby, turned it upside down, hit it on the back, and the baby was sick and then cried. The mother always said he had saved her daughter's life.

'When delivering Christmas orders, it was very difficult to refuse "just a glass of my home-made wine and a mince pie". There were no drink and drive laws then or it would have been easier. The wine certainly kept me warm when putting sacks under the back wheels of the van to drive out of the deep snow.

*Kathleen Edwards helping with the milk float
pulled by Gypsy, a popular horse
with all the children of Coleshill,
in the early 1950s.
(Lindsey Haubner – Coleshill)*

*Coleshill milkman Douglas Pusey doing his round
in 1965, now with a van,
and helped this time by
Brian and Alan Edwards.
His is the only vehicle to be seen in
Hill Meadow.
(Lindsey Haubner – Coleshill)*

There seemed to be more snow then and in the winter we always carried sacks and a shovel to dig out of deep snow.'

At Coleshill in the Fifties, *Lindsey Haubner* agreed, delivery men were an essential part of life. 'Apart from the one village store, which sold most things, from paraffin to foodstuffs, to fishing nets for catching tiddlers in the pond, there were several delivery people. A haberdashery van came from London on Fridays; there was a grocer in Amersham who would come round and take your order one day and deliver a couple of days later; Stevens Butchers delivered, and there were two bakers and an ironmonger. Dairy goods could be bought straight from several farms which were still being worked in the village, as could potatoes or cherries at certain times.'

Service was not dead in the Sixties, either. *Beryl Hulbert (Oakley)* thought a wonderful old custom in the village when she moved there was 'the once-a-week single decker bus to Oxford', with its helpful driver. We would stop all along the way picking people up at houses, not necessarily by a bus stop, or collecting items for cleaning or repair. For example, one week we stopped outside a cottage on the way home and the driver took in a pair of shoes to the old lady there. "I dropped them off at the shoemenders in Headington last week for her," he told me, "ready this week." Such a friendly helpful world we lived in!'

CHAPTER FIVE
GETTING ABOUT

*'In post-war Coleshill, people still mostly walked or cycled, so a trip
to the village shop, church or school would have time allowed for several
chats along the way. Very little traffic used the lanes and it was safe for
quite young children to visit friends or walk to school without danger.'*

(Lindsey Haubner – Coleshill)

C ars have been a mixed blessing in our lives. We have gained a
freedom of movement that our grandparents never knew, but we
have lost forever those quiet, safe lanes and roads.

'The old A355, which ran from Amersham to Beaconsfield, was a very
winding lane until the early 1960s when the new road was built. Lengths of
the old lane can still be seen in the form of lay-bys, often used by travellers
who nowadays leave them in a dreadful state but were then more careful. Kiln
Farm, near the water tower, had to be sacrificed and was completely cleared to
make way for the new road. One of our members can remember driving into
Beaconsfield in the 1950s and remarking to her husband that she had seen
three other cars on her journey, and this was quite busy for then. By the late
1980s, the new road was so busy that drivers were already using our village as
a "rat run" and pedestrians have, still, to be very careful, but then cars were
rare in the village.' *(Lindsey Haubner, Coleshill)*

FIRST CAR

Vera German (Stony Stratford) can remember her first car very clearly. She worked as a Health Visitor during the war and needed to drive for her work with schoolchildren, families and evacuees.

After just three driving lessons, Vera collected a second-hand car from Bedford and began work. She received petrol coupons from the Health Authority so that she could carry out her work. Rules about using petrol for private use were strict. You had to make the shortest possible journey to get anywhere, or you would be wasting petrol.

Vera only broke the rules once – on VE Day, when the war was finally over and she went to join in with the celebrations.

Shortly after the war, Vera gave up work to start a family and put her car on the market. New cars had not been made for years and people were eager to get hold of them. It was a good time to sell. 'I bought the Ford for £35 and sold it for £112!'

Children in the 1950s rarely travelled by car, usually only on special occasions. 'One day after school,' recalled *Carole Bowler (Hazlemere Evening)*, 'we set off to Naphill for Ian Simpson's birthday party – seven kids squeezed into his father's little black Austin. As the car turned the sharp corner to go up to Coombe Lane, Ian must have pressed

Vera German and her first car, a Ford, in 1948. Note the car doors opened the opposite way to today.
(Vera German – Stony Stratford)

on the chain handle and unnoticed by his father, rolled out into the gutter. Fortunately, Ian was well-upholstered and when he had caught up with us, we all went on our way laughing.

'Although my father travelled daily to work on his moped (later a Vespa) we were fortunate enough to own a family car which was kept only for special or long journeys. Church was considered special enough and we travelled the four miles there and back most Sundays, also visiting my paternal grandmother in Highgate once a month.'

Avril Hartin (Downley Evening) agreed that 'using public transport was the norm, as I didn't have access to a car as my father never learnt to drive or owned one. My first encounter came at 16 when I met my future husband. His father had a car and I thought they were loaded!'

GETTING THE CHILDREN TO SCHOOL

'We arrived in July 1946 to a house on the outskirts of Chalfont St Peter – still a smallish village – and quickly found places for the two older children to start school in September. These were both in Gerrards Cross, about two miles away,' wrote *Janet Cross (Horn Hill)*.

'The great problem was transport because, although we had a car, my husband took it to work every day. Andrew went by bicycle, and continued to do so until he left at the age of twelve to go to Merchant Taylors – I doubt whether anyone would allow a seven year old to bike on his own these days, but he came to no harm.

'There was a bus service about a quarter of a mile from us to Gerrards Cross, and I walked Hilary to the stop. I gave the conductor the penny for Hilary's fare, and asked him to put her off at the nearest stop to the school, having first taken her to see the short walk to school. I asked the teacher to make sure Hilary left in time for the return journey and put a penny in her coat pocket and a note, "Get off at Gravel Hill". All went well most of the time, but there were some difficult occasions. Once she came off the bus in tears, having lost her penny. A kind lady had paid for her with two ha'pennies but Hilary had not realised that that was the same as a penny.

'Another time I was late at the bus stop, As Hilary was not waiting for me, I presumed the bus was late, and was amazed when a bus coming from the opposite direction, stopped and put her down. The conductor had realised she had gone too far, hailed an oncoming bus, swapped the child and given instructions to drop her at Gravel Hill. I cannot imagine such a service these days.'

WE WALKED OR CYCLED!

'Still in the mid to late 1950s villagers walked or cycled to Marston Gate to catch a train to Aylesbury,' points out *Wingrave WI*. 'At the beginning of the war the local garage owner ran a bus to Aylesbury and some-times when it was wet, transported the children from Rowsham to the village school in Wingrave to save a wet and muddy walk through the fields. Many workers cycled to Aylesbury.

'When snow in 1963 blocked the road through the village, we walked to the main road to fetch milk. There we

In 1958 you could be 'gay, glamorous and happy' on a bicycle'!

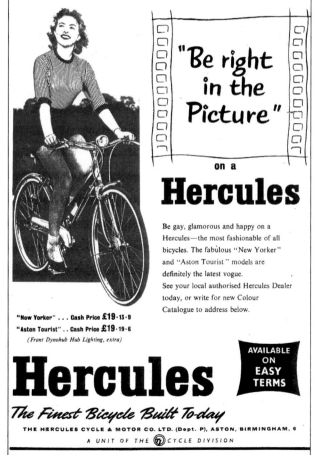

"Be right in the Picture"

on a

Hercules

Be gay, glamorous and happy on a Hercules—the most fashionable of all bicycles. The fabulous "New Yorker" and "Aston Tourist" models are definitely the latest vogue.
See your local authorised Hercules Dealer today, or write for new Colour Catalogue to address below.

"New Yorker" . . . Cash Price £19·13·9
"Aston Tourist" . . Cash Price £19·19·6
(Front Dynohub Hub Lighting, extra)

AVAILABLE ON EASY TERMS

Hercules
The Finest Bicycle Built To-day

THE HERCULES CYCLE & MOTOR CO. LTD. (Dept. P), ASTON, BIRMINGHAM, 6
A UNIT OF THE Ⓗ CYCLE DIVISION

found a number of cars had had to be abandoned – their owners walking home!'

THE INFLUENCE OF THE CAR

'I have lived in Hanslope all my life. Ironically, the pre-war population was in the order of 1,000 but at that time we had 22 shops and businesses in the village, making us self-sufficient. In addition to the shops, home deliveries by the butcher, baker, fishmonger, the mobile Co-op shop, the farmer's milk delivery and the coal merchant were the norm. Gradually since 1945 the village population has increased to 4,000 while at the same time our service businesses have been reduced to a combined grocer/post office, a newsagent, a butcher, a draper, a wine merchant, a pet food shop and a shop selling pine furniture and ornaments. A testimony,' *Barbara Bellham (Hanslope)* goes on, 'to the influence of the motor car which takes people outside the village for major supplies.

'How would the motor car have fared in 1947, the year of the "big freeze"? Hanslope was cut off for almost a week and all the able-bodied men were asked to help dig out a road from Hanslope to Castlethorpe Station so that coal could be brought into the village.'

WONDERFUL STEAM TRAINS

Trains evoke so many affectionate memories. Steam trains were a part of our lives in a way the modern diesel trains have never managed to be.

'Going by train was so good,' said *Pamela Allen (Winslow)*. 'We would go on the steam train from Winslow to Bletchley, and the smoke billowed under the bridges as we rode along. Children waved. Our pram went into the guards van and it was all much more convenient than a bus.

'At Bletchley station the trains would roar by to all sorts of destinations – the Flying Scotsman, the Mallard, the Sir Nigel Gresley, such wonderful names. They always shone in the sunlight. The mail train stopped at Bletchley for loading and then went on its way to Scotland.

'If you were on the platform when an express passed you, you had to hold your ears, as the noise was deafening. And you came away with black smuts

The mobile shop was once a common sight in Buckinghamshire villages.

on you. Some trains had corridors and compartments off them you could have to yourself but others just had single compartments. Some had "Ladies Only" carriages!'

END OF AN ERA

In 1952, *Ruth Potts (Templewood and Hedgerley)* witnessed the end of an era.

'There is a single-line railway track that runs from Slough railway station and carries a smart two-carriage train, bearing tourists towards the attractions of nearby Windsor.

'At one stage it passes the playground of the Slough and Eton Secondary Modern School which, in 1952, was in the county of Buckinghamshire.

'In those far-off schooldays of mine, an old engine pulling two carriages used to clatter along that track so frequently that its progress marked the start and end of play-time and the periods between lessons. To everyone at the school and to those living nearby, this train was known affectionately as the Chalvey Flyer.

'However, for one day in 1952, everything changed.

'For that day, pupils were asked to attend school in either proper school uniform or, if appropriate, in Boy Scout, Girl Guide or Boy's Brigade uniform.

'During the day we were solemnly led out into the playground by sombrely dressed teachers, and lined up in straight rows, facing the railway line. When the time came we were ordered to salute if we belonged to one of the aforementioned groups, or to stand smartly to attention with our heads bowed.

'A train approached slowly, travelling almost at walking pace. It was not our own Chalvey Flyer, but a sleek and shiny black engine pulling three sleek and shiny black coaches. The first and third coaches had their window blinds down.

'The middle coach, draped in mourning cloth, carried the body of King

Bletchley was a busy station in the days of steam. (Pamela Allen – Winslow)

George VI on his final journey to Windsor Castle for his interment in St George's Chapel.

'We schoolchildren were witnessing the end of an era, and the beginning of the New Elizabethan Age.'

THE OLD CHESHAM SHUTTLE

Barbara Chapman (Chesham and Ashley Green) looks back to the days of the 'Chesham Shuttle'.

'"You sound just like the Chesham Shuttle", said a friend as I pulled my shopping trolley over the cobblestones in King Street. I was immediately reminded of the days when I lived in Little Chalfont and used to take my children to Chesham for a great treat, a day in the park. We had to travel in the guards' van on the Chesham branch line as I had a pram for the baby and two other children. The rest of the train was all small compartments, where six people sat facing six others. There were sepia photos of the area and, above, fishnet-type luggage racks. Each of the compartments had a separate door which had to be banged shut and there were thick leather straps to raise and lower the windows.

'This line was the very last stretch of "underground" railway to be electrified, and this happened in 1960. The week before the little engine was pensioned off for ever, we took our last journey in the guards' van. It was a very unpleasant if memorable experience, as one of the former occupants of the van that day had obviously been a load of very smelly fish!

'People are amazed when I tell them that until the mid-fifties the train used to spend about five minutes at Rickmansworth Station changing from an electric to a steam engine. The spare ones used to be on a siding on the London side of the station, steamed up ready to be hitched up to the train. In those days every other train went up the branch line to Watford so you had to be sure you were on the right train.

'It was certainly an experience to travel on the Metropolitan Railway in the past.'

CHAPTER SIX
A LAND GIRL IN LITTLE HAMPDEN

Land girls were a familiar sight during the war in country districts, filling the jobs on farms vacated by men called up for the Services and proving themselves an essential part of the war effort. However, land girls did not disappear with the end of the war – they were still needed in the post-war years, as *Frankie Westlake (Great Hampden)* recalls. She was destined to return to Little Hampden where she was billeted from 1945 to 1947, as a married woman with a young family in 1962.

'My first sight of Little Hampden was in the summer of 1945. I was being taken by the local "man from the Ministry" of Agriculture and Fisheries to Little Hampden House, a large residence that had been leased, for a peppercorn rent, to the Women's Land Army. It was a billet for 24 land girls. I was 18 years old and a very new recruit.

'Coming from a large northern city, the narrow winding country lanes that led to the house and village, seemed a world away. Another girl and I piled out of the small van, gathered our kit, of which there was rather a lot, and presented ourselves at the main entrance of the house.

'The lady who greeted us was very refined looking; white haired, extremely elegant and in her mid seventies. I learned later she had been Warden of Baker Street YWCA before taking up her post at Little Hampden House. Her assistant I only ever knew as Amy. There were four Irish maids and a man who did the gardening and odd jobs around the house.

'The warden – Mrs Hardwicke – took our ration books and employment cards, allocated us bunks and a place to stow our gear, and told us never to use the front door again. Her parting shot was, "Dinner is being served when you are ready", leaving my colleague and I slightly bemused.

'The following day I was taken to a nearby farm. As a member of the "thrashing gang" (six girls) I was initiated into one of the filthiest jobs on a farm – chaff clearer.

'By the end of the week I had explored the rest of the village and discovered it was mentioned in the Domesday Book. It comprised three farmhouses – Hampden Bottom, Manor and Little Hampden Farms – a Manor House, three large houses, 19 smaller homes, a pub and a Saxon church. The pub was reputed to have been a haunt of the highwayman, Dick Turpin.

'The Rector of Great and Little Hampden was Mr Bamford, a saintly old parson, who lived like a hermit. He quoted Shakespeare at the drop of a hat and as far as I recall, rarely followed a service to the letter.

'The church organist was farm manager and eventually became my boss, for after working six weeks as a member of the thrashing gang, I heard there was an opening for a milker at Little Hampden Farm. Part of the estate owned by Sir Clifford Figg, it comprised over 300 acres of arable and woodland. The fields were surrounded by mainly beechwoods and were a joy to behold the year round, taking on a different mantle with every season.

'Working amongst the villagers, I was lucky enough to come to know them all. When cows calved I usually distributed the "beastings" (first milk) to the local ladies, who made it into a kind of pudding. And of course there was the skimmed milk after the milk was separated for butter making. Extra milk was always welcome.

'By today's standards the work was primitive. The milking, at first, was by hand, but later a small petrol engine was installed to power two machines (due to a herd increase). Cows were mostly large horned Ayrshires (de-horning was not a common practice). Tractors offered no protection and the hard metal seats were most uncomfortable. No protective masks were on offer at harvest time or when spreading fertilizer from a box that bounced behind the tractor.

'Little Hampden is about two miles from Great Missenden and the railway station. There were few car owners so a bike was very much the means of travel. I hired a bike for a shilling a month from the WLA. Saturdays and Sundays would find large groups of girls cycling along Rignall Road – also used, amongst others, by the Prime Minister on his way to Chequers.

'The first Saturday I joined about 20 other girls and set off for Great Missenden. We were allowed to leave our bikes at Readings Farm, and caught the London train. It stopped at many places en route for the city, and the first was Amersham. This town boasted one of the few Service canteens open to land girls. We were not an armed service, was the reason given by NAAFI for our exclusion from the others.

'On the return journey that evening, after a visit to the cinema, I was riding in the middle of the group along the pitch black lane when suddenly, from out of the shadows, someone stepped in front of me and shone a powerful torch in my eyes. The end of the war in Europe had meant the ending of blackout restrictions, and a voice demanded to know where my lamps were. I had no idea it was against the law to ride in the dark without them. To make matters worse, the owner of the voice was the local police sergeant and he wished to see my identity card too – it was back at the hostel. The outcome was I received a summons to appear at the local Magistrates Court and was fined eight shillings. Because it was a Wednesday and I was out of funds, I had to ask for time to pay. Our wages were £2 2s 0d per week and we paid £1 9s 0d for board and lodging. The remainder funded all our other needs, fares, civvy clothes, sweets, toilet gear and entertainment. A brief item appeared the following week in the local newspaper headed "Lampless Landgirl".

'After two years I left the WLA, though I always kept in touch with Mr and Mrs Burton, never dreaming that one day I would return to Little Hampden. In 1962 my husband, an ex-naval man, heard there was work for him and we moved in to Manor Farm, which had been converted into two houses. We had two young boys and it was early spring. A good time to start a new life.

'There had been quite a few changes in the village. Church Cottage was transformed into a much larger and more modern building. The old ship barn (built from the hull of an 18th century ship) was extended to house grain dryers and tractors. A large milking parlour and dairy stood on the rise of the hill between Manor and Little Hampden Farm. Most of the villagers were still there, though some had changed houses and one had "come up on the Pools" and left. The pub had a new landlord and the Manor House was a boys' preparatory school. Old Revd Bamford had gone to his maker, and the Revd Percy Hill served the two parishes. The farm manager still played the organ and Mr Leonard Figg had inherited after the death of his father. Still no buses, but tradesmen called once a week. Bikes were still our means of transport and I made sure we all had lights fixed for night riding!'

CHAPTER SEVEN
CHILDHOOD MEMORIES

'Life was safer in those days. I let my little girls play alone in the nearby woods, and later, when they were both at the same school, they walked up a narrow footpath from the bus stop to our house – I would not do either myself now!'

(Janet Cross – Horn Hill)

Growing up in the Forties and Fifties, we have fond memories of our comics, sweets and games, but we also found enjoyment in a freedom to wander the lanes and fields that sadly has been lost to many of us today. It was still a childhood world that our parents would have recognised – and the 'teenager' was only just arriving on the scene.

It is often said that 'we made our own fun', though as *Jean Brinded (Wingrave)* pointed out, that was because we had to. 'We didn't have many sweets, we were lucky if we had a penny to spend every other day, but as every other child was the same we didn't worry.'

'My favourite comics were the Beano and Dandy, and reading them every week and eating sticks of penny liquorice was absolute heaven. My toys were quite sparse, my doll called Susan and a real Rupert Bear and a very small tin doll's pram were my favourites. Everything else was kept in two shoeboxes and to this day my most personal possessions are kept in boxes,' said *Avril Hartin (Downley Evening)*. How many children do you know today who could get their toys into two shoeboxes!

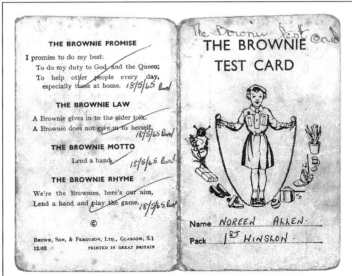

Winslow Brownies in 1965, and the Brownie Test Card. (Pamela Allen – Winslow)

SUNNY DAYS

'My childhood memories are of long sunny days, helping with the haymaking, all friends and neighbours taking part,' wrote *Prudence Goodwin (Wingrave).*

'Very cold winters, deep snow and the excitement of the village being cut off. The suffering of painful chilblains, all huddled very cosily round the coal and wood fire and not wanting to move out of the room to face the cold hall, bedrooms and bathroom. Wearing liberty bodices with rubber buttons. Chilprufe vests, gym slips, long socks and long navy knickers with a white lining because of the dye in the navy material.

'Saturday morning errands, and housework before we were allowed out to play. Taking the shopping list to the local shop, which always began "Butter, sugar, marg, lard…"

'Sunday school and chapel a must. We were the "Meths", real competition

Prams were still made to last – and the wheels made a great go-cart later! (Pamela Allen – Winslow)

with the Church and the "Congs". Sunday we were never allowed to knit or embroider, just read and play records on the gramophone which needed winding up after playing two sides.

'When we had chickenpox, whooping cough or measles we were made a great fuss of, with a fire in the bedroom and lots of goodies, and for me relief knowing I had three weeks off school. My favourite comic was School Friend, and my favourite books the Famous Five series by Enid Blyton.

'When sweets were rationed, I remember cutting a Mars bar into seven pieces to last the week. And deciding that rather than pool all our sweets in a white enamel tin on the kitchen shelf and share with my sisters, I would have my own. That only lasted a week as I had eaten my allowance by Tuesday.'

SUNDAY SCHOOL

Prudence was not the only one whose memories of childhood included regular attendance at Sunday school. 'I went to Sunday school twice and then chapel twice every Sunday. We thought nothing of that as it was what we were brought up to do,' said *Mrs D. Bignell (Wingrave)*.

Pamela Allen (Winslow) remembers it vividly. 'Sunday school – Sunday afternoon at 2 pm, with a red coat on with black velvet collar and cuffs to match, long socks and lace-up brown shoes. A large white ribbon on one side of the head, with short hair. I hated short hair. I still do.'

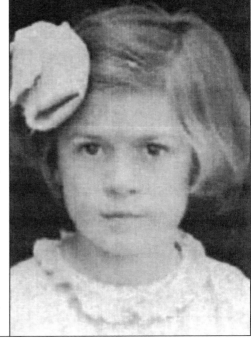

Pamela Allen in the 1950s. Pamela Allen – Winslow)

A BOY IN THE FORTIES

'When I was a boy in Wingrave, in the forties, I can remember when the pond and the moat at the bottom of the rec (recreation ground) used to freeze over, and we used to play ice hockey on the pond, with sticks made from elderberry branches and a tennis ball for a puck.

'On the moat, which was full of grass at the bottom end near the Anchor, we would run along as fast as we could, and the ice would bounce up and down because of the grass in it – a bit like a water bed I suppose. The top end of the moat was deep and I don't remember that it froze hard enough for us to play on.

'In the late spring and summer, the grassy end of the moat had clumps of kingcups in it.

Meccano sets were prized gifts for many boys – Andrew Cross made an electric magnetic crane with his in 1950. (Janet Cross – Horn Hill)

'We played with iron hoops and sticks about the village and, when they broke, we used to go to Tommy Woodruff, the blacksmith, to get them hammer welded – he made both ends red hot and hammered them together good as new.

'On hot summer days we'd walk down to Mill Bridge, on the footpath between Rowsham and Hulcott. There was a fairly deep bit of brook there we used to go and bathe in. When the village show time came there was a class for children for wild flower arrangements, which we used to enter and we got a lot of our flowers and grasses from down there – whatever was in season. Course, we always used to help out with haymaking and harvest at Windmill Hill Farm and Mitchell Leys. Michael Higgins at Windmill Hill would acquire old lorry chassis and convert them into trailers for the farms. At Mitchell Leys there were still two working horses, Jim and George, and I was allowed to take them up and down from the harvest field to bring the hay and corn in.

'Just off Dean Leys, between Dean Leys and Castle Street, Dodder Gibbs had an orchard and there was a particular special apple tree in it with a notice on one autumn to say "please do not steal these apples, they are for the Harvest Festival". Someone (we know not who) stole the apples (all the lot) and left behind another notice saying, "all is safely gathered in".

'We helped at the threshing too, in the wartime. The threshing equipment was towed from farm to farm; it belonged to a contractor. They used to put a wire net fence round the bottom of the rick before we started and us boys and the farm terriers – two dogs and two bitches – would patrol the bit between the wire and the rick and kill any rats that came out. At Windmill Hill, they always had a couple of foxhound puppies at walk – socialising them before they joined the hunt.

'During the war a tank got ditched down the Marston road and there weren't a lot of breakdown vehicles about – a couple of tractors in the village but they weren't powerful enough to pull it out. But there was a big steamroller working down the road on road repairs so they brought that up, hooked a chain on it, the man opened the steam valve on the roller and it pulled the tank up out of the ditch like a cork out of a bottle. No effort at all. Mother came home excited one day – reckoned she'd seen a motor cycle with a tin hat on it. It was the rider she meant. We had a good laugh at that.' *Dennis Lambourne (via Wingrave)*

CHILDHOOD MEMORIES OF WINTERS PAST

'The "Underwood" behind Underwood Cottages was the source of many imaginative games once the leaves had fallen in the autumn. My favourite was bunching the leaves up into long lines to form walls of imaginary homes. We would then visit each others' houses, pretending to be in the scullery, bedroom, or front room (the best room). Friends who were lucky enough to have a bag of broken biscuits would share these out to "entertain their guests".

'Looking back, winters seemed much harder and journeys through thick snow were quite a feat. I especially remember the mile walk to Coleshill school where the snow drifts were so high that they would completely fill the lane and we would actually find ourselves walking over the hedge-tops.

'The common had at this time a pond called "the pit" – originally dug for clay-making at the kiln where now the Potters Arms is situated. In the winter this was the scene of much activity where children would slide across from one side to the other. We didn't have such luxuries as skates – but the thrill of who dared to cross the centre and deepest part was enough for us. We all knew that a child had once drowned in the pit and it was forbidden by most parents to go near it, so we were skating on thin ice in more ways than one.

'The steep hill in the field behind the Queen's Head was used as a toboggan run by children. Being the heaviest of my group of friends I was always sent down first to see how far the sledge would go. Unfortunately, I would sometimes end up in the hedge, and on one occasion I can remember going home to my mum to have the hawthorn prickles removed from my bottom!

'As a child I was unaware that we were quite poor but, looking back now, I realise that we were. Generally I was quite content with my lot but I do remember being envious of my dear friend Margaret Tarry who lived at Luckings Farm, who always had a new coat every winter. I remember the joy when Betty (another dear friend), Margaret and I all had new coats one winter, I really felt I'd "arrived".' *Greta Reading (Winchmore Hill).*

VARIOUS DELIGHTS

'The journey of two miles home from school afforded various delights to young children eager for adventure,' recalled *Carole Bowler (Hazlemere)*. 'First call on a cold day was at the forge to watch the blacksmith and feel the fireglow. Nearby was Mr James's shop where we would call for our penny sherbet dabs or gobstoppers. Our headmistress, Miss Cordelia Snell, would send the older children there daily for her cigarettes. The opposite side of the road was Tuckers Dump and jumping over the sandpits all the way down the long hill gave us healthy exercise. In the spring whilst searching for tadpoles we would crawl along the culvert right under the main Hughenden Road and emerge the other side near the stream where we had a secret camp in some old willow trees.

'In the school holidays we were given a picnic and set off for the day to Hughenden Park, meeting other children en route. The greatest attraction was Horseshoe Pond and one memorable day one of the older children let us have a paddle across the water to the island, in the inner tube of a lorry. Many summer days were spent on the nearby farm, assisting with haymaking or hanging over the pigsty doors watching a new litter of piglets – we avoided Charlie the huge bad-tempered boar. We went home with swollen eyes and itching bodies at haytime, but happily exhausted. We loved to watch the hand milking in the dairy and it was a great disappointment when the electric machines appeared.'

ANGELIC IN THE CHOIR

'The year was 1958. I knew he was looking at me. Although I had my head bowed, I could still feel his glare. I nudged my friend by my side and she looked up and saw him. Now he was pointing at me. She whispered in my ear to look up. I shook my head and closed my eyes even tighter.

'The "Amen" finally came. When I looked up he had a look of devilment in his eyes. It was so hard to ignore him. Then I noticed his hand in his pocket. What did he have this time?

'It was the same every Sunday at Family Communion at St Mark's church, Bourne End,' wrote *Linda Axford (Haddenham Witchert)*. 'I was trying to be angelic in my front row position in the choir. The girls on one side with the organ behind us and the boys opposite. Although there were wooden pillars between us and the congregation, I'm sure they could see what was going on.

'At this stage the Vicar was giving his usual long and boring sermon, which of course was the perfect opportunity for "him" to take advantage. He started to wriggle in his seat causing the other boys to take notice ... then they started sniggering as he took his hand out of his pocket. One of the senior members cleared his throat, meaning "Quiet please". Then we heard it – a distinct croak and the boys shifted in their seats. By now we had the giggles. It was hard to stop our bodies from shaking. They had a baby frog and it had obviously jumped from his hand onto their bare knees.

'The Vicar continued unaware of what was going on behind him. The frog escaped and hid behind the altar and the boys settled down. Time for hymns now and the old organ had to be pumped by hand. Each boy took turns each Sunday to do this.

'I loved being in the choir and looked forward to every Tuesday evening for choir practice. When I got home from school Mum had always bought a fresh crusty loaf which was thickly buttered to go with our baked beans. My friend called for me and off we trotted at 6.30 in the evening to church. The boys were shown how to pump the organ, but at the actual service "he" always did it too fast causing the organist to lose the tempo and hit the wrong notes.

'He was always very special in my life. He became my first boyfriend and has been like a brother every since. Those old days of going to church every Sunday were good. We still misbehaved but we had a great sense of belonging. My parents weren't particularly religious but it was the done thing in those days to go to church. We always wore our Sunday best – and I remember my knitted bonnet which had a hairband in it and a bobble at the back. My gloves were on elastic which went round my back so I couldn't lose them, and I had "sensible" shoes. The vicars in those days were usually single and we called them Father, and sometimes we were invited to their homes for tea!'

CHAPTER EIGHT
Schooldays

'There was more discipline at school than there is now, which was a good thing. We learned to respect our teachers and the police. We obeyed them and our parents too.'

(Jean Brinded – Wingrave)

Most of us went to small local schools and would recognise the description of the headmaster at Wingrave: 'The headmaster (1919–1950) was stern and very well respected. He used to know, by the beginning of school the next morning, of misbehaviour the previous evening, and the child had a very strict telling off in front of the whole school in assembly. When you met him in the street you addressed him as "Sir". To use as a cane on the boys he cut a piece from the lilac tree; the girls just lost their playtime.' *Mrs D. Bignell (Wingrave)* confirms that 'it was much stricter than it is now. We were very wary of the teachers.'

WARTIME SCHOOLDAYS

Irene Smith (Winslow) never forgot one particular lesson. 'One morning before he began school assembly, my headmaster held up one small toffee paper and said casually, "I found this in the top corridor this morning. Neither I nor the school want it. Will the owner please come and collect it."

'I considered that he had delivered his homily and that was the end of the matter. Immediately the sound of crisp footsteps were heard. From the back of the entire assembled school came one of the youngest boys and picked up the paper. The head caught his gaze and began to smile with admiration and, I suspect, a feeling that he was the one left looking silly! He began to applaud the lad and the school cheered heartily.

'I often think of this incident when I see litter strewn everywhere, especially food wrappers. Some people seem to eat anytime and anywhere. At this same school the senior mistress made sure that we never "ate in the street". Even today I feel slightly uncomfortable when I lick an ice cream at the seaside.'

Irene began her schooldays during the war, which produced problems of its own. Then she progressed to Wolverton Grammar School in 1949, and this time it was the lack of transport that was 'somewhat problematic'!

'When I started school in 1940, of the two dozen or so pupils several had to make their way from outlying farms. One day I was given a lift in a military truck and really rode high.

'Occasionally the postman would take me into the village. Sometimes there were rabbits in the van which had been posted by country people to their

Winslow school pupils in the late 1940s.
(Pamela Allen – Winslow)

BUCKS COUNTY EDUCATION COMMITTEE

——————◆◆——————

Secondary Schools Entrance Examination
Friday, 21st March, 1941.

——————◆◆——————

ARITHMETIC—PART II.

Time : 40 minutes. From 9.35 a.m. to 10.15 a.m.

Put the number of the question in the margin, and show all your working or marks may be lost.

1.—Divide £36 0s. 9¼d. by 29.

2.—Out of 150,000 unemployed persons, 64,137 were men, 39,484 were boys and girls under the age of 18 years, and the rest were women. How many more men than women were unemployed ?

3.—£43 18s. 3d. is divided among 21 men and 18 women, giving each of the men £1 more than each woman. How much does each man and each woman receive ?

4.—At the end of the day a shopkeeper found he had taken 96 halfpennies, 243 pennies, 197 sixpences, 135 shillings, 85 florins, 69 half-crowns, and 3 ten shilling notes. What was the total of the day's takings ?

5.—A seedsman weighed 13 cwt. 1 qr. of artificial manure into bags each containing 3½ lb. and sold them at 1s. 4½d. per bag. How much did he receive altogether ?

6.—How long will it take a man to walk 9 miles if he takes on an average 120 steps, each 2 ft. 3 ins. every minute ?

7.—Full daylight begins half an hour before sunrise and lasts until half an hour after sunset. On 1st March sunrise is at 6.46 a.m. and sunset is at 5.40 p.m. On 8th March sunrise is 15 minutes earlier and sunset is 12 minutes later than on 1st March. How many hours, etc. of full daylight are there on 8th March ?

The Arithmetic paper for 1941 in the Secondary Schools Entrance Exam. (Irene Smith — Winslow) friends in the towns. This was permitted so long as the heads were securely wrapped. Once, when it was raining "cats and dogs" the laundry roundsman called at the school just before hometime and asked permission to take me and my sister home.

'The school had no telephone and neither did we. Once, I walked to school and found the gates locked and all very quiet. For some reason which I have forgotten there was no school that day. The only time the sole teacher was ill, an older boy was sent to meet us to tell us that the school had been closed.

'We used to take a packed lunch which we ate in the infants' room under the supervision of the infants' teacher, who had a long cycle ride to work. She used to knit and read during the lunch break. I remember one time when the munching of sandwiches in the silence became too much for me and I had a fit of the giggles. I was scolded and sent next door to the empty juniors room where I continued to giggle. Later there was a period when my sister and I were the only pupils left taking a packed lunch. The school by this time was a one-teacher school so we were left in the building whilst the teacher went to her home immediately opposite to have her lunch.

'When I had finished eating I would delve with glee into the Country Library box of children's books. At a later time when I had a bicycle I alternated between the two generous grandmothers for lunch. One lived at Pear Tree Farm in the High Street and the other lived in a lone cottage on the Nash borders. I would whizz down the Nash hill on June days anticipating stewed strawberries and creamy custard. The haul up the hill afterwards was not so enjoyable.

'We paid twopence halfpenny per week for milk which was brought to school daily by one of the pupils. The milk was inspected regularly and I remember the inspector saying on one occasion that the milk was all right but we did need to replace the can.

'Young soldiers stationed in the village would sometimes waylay the boys and ask them if they had any comics to spare. Perhaps Desperate Dan, Pansy Potter, Weary Willie and Tired Tim made a contribution to the war effort. Who knows! A uniformed lady called in school one day to ask us to collect empty cotton reels to cover cables. Once we were urged to gather rosehips for syrup. Regularly, I think it was every month, I would collect our quota of concentrated orange juice and cod liver oil from the village.

'Popular Reverend Oliver from Mursley used to pay an annual visit to conduct a Scripture examination and award the Bishop's Prize. The vicar also called from time to time. He spoke of activity on a Sunday as being "healthy recreation" and far from wicked. At the time this was radical thinking.

'A school photographer came. We had virtually no accommodation for tidying ourselves. Our toilets were the bucket variety ...

'Finally, I recall this incident. A girl brought to school one day some attractive magazine cutouts of Fred Astaire and Ginger Rogers and asked if she could put them on the wall. After a slight hesitation the head replied: "Oh, very well. They will help to keep the walls together."

'Things are better today.

'When I started at Wolverton Grammar School in 1949 my journey to and from was somewhat problematic as my family still, like many others, had neither car nor telephone.

'I lived at a farm on the edge of Whaddon parish so cycled into that village to catch a school bus that took pupils as far as the Stony Stratford schools. As they piled into their classrooms I had to catch a public service bus for Wolverton. After alighting I then had to walk through an alley to the grammar school. Thus I was late every day, missing assembly and notices. I had to ask my classmates what was said and, not surprisingly, they were bored sometimes.

'At the end of the school day I was obliged to leave before the last lesson in order to catch a public service bus back to the Stony Stratford schools, to board the school bus for the return journey to the villages.

'An elderly ex-military gentleman on the North Bucks Education Committee realised that something had to be done for children who lived "in the sticks". At his suggestion a boarding hostel was established in the same building as the area education office (this house had formerly been the childhood home of Bishop Hapgood – it is now a restaurant). Now I missed only Monday morning assembly and last lesson on Friday – not ideal but getting better!

O 1(a)

OXFORD LOCAL EXAMINATIONS

GENERAL CERTIFICATE OF EDUCATION

Summer Examination, 1951

Ordinary Level

ENGLISH LANGUAGE, PAPER (a)

THURSDAY, JUNE 28. TIME ALLOWED—1 HOUR

[Write the number of the paper, O 1 (a), on the left at the head of each sheet of your answers in the space provided.

Special attention must be paid to spelling, punctuation and the construction of sentences.

Remember that soundness of style and suitability of material are much more important than mere length. You should write a composition covering about two sides of the writing-paper, if your writing is of average size (i.e. seven to nine words to a line). In any case your composition must not exceed three sides of the writing-paper.]

Either, (*a*) Write a composition on **one** of the following subjects:

(i) Unwelcome visitors.

(ii) Do you consider that Physical Training in the gymnasium should take the place of school games?

Or, (*b*) Write an answer to a person who asks, 'Why waste your time reading poetry?'

Or, (*c*) Describe the making of a new road or the widening of an old road which you have seen taking place.

Or, (*d*) You have been asked to make a speech about your own school to a party of foreigners who understand English. Write the speech you would make.

51 A 1

In 1951 the first
GCE examinations
were set.
(Irene Smith –
Winslow)

'One Friday, when I was about 14, I was waiting outside the Stratford schools for the bus home, and there was an unusually quiet air. After some time a woman, whose daughter was in my form, opened her front door and called, "Are you waiting for the school bus?"

"Yes," I replied.

"Well," she said, "there isn't one today. The Stony Stratford schools have had a holiday."

'The door closed.

'It was too far to walk home, especially with a case and satchel. At 5.30 pm the Carriage and Wagon Works at Wolverton closed and the men poured into the streets, returning home on foot, by bicycle, and some – by bus! At 5.40 pm there would be a Works bus leaving Stony Stratford for all the villages as far as Whaddon. I resolved to catch it.

'I had to wait over an hour and a half. When the bus arrived, I boarded it and made for the only empty seat right behind the driver's cab and breathed a sigh of relief. The clippie and I were the only females.

'At Whaddon I then set out to walk the last mile or so home, wondering what my parents were thinking about the delay. After about five minutes I saw my father coming to meet me. Nothing much was said. He saw I was all right.'

A VERY BIG STEP

'It was the year 1945 and I was to go to the Aylesbury Grammar School in September. At that time to go from a small almost one-big-family school, in a village, to a much larger school in a town was a very big step, far greater than the distance of five or six miles suggested.

'A school uniform must be bought and worn from the start. Clothes were "on coupons" but I seem to recall that we had a coupon allowance for the purpose. What I do know for sure is that because I had large feet I needed to go to Mr Stubbs, the then headmaster at Wingrave School, to display my feet and have them accurately measured, to prove to him that they were well above the average, which enabled him to apply for me to have "extra coupons".

However, coupons or not, large black lace-up shoes for girls were not to be found anywhere within our shopping radius. Time was running out and the decision was made that I must purchase and wear boys' shoes. Yes, they were black. Yes, they were lace-ups. But they were not comfortable.

'The day to start at my new school arrived. The travelling arrangements were that I walked from the village to the Handpost (now known as Wingrave Crossroads), the best part of a mile, in order to catch an 8.30 am bus which came from Bedford. The bus was already crowded on arrival; office workers, shop assistants and schoolchildren were all making their way into Aylesbury for 9 o'clock and invariably the schoolchildren stood for the journey. I then clambered from the bus at Park Street to walk down, at fast pace, to the grammar school, again the best part of a mile, to arrive as close to 9 o'clock as possible.

The Queen opening Rivers County Infants School in Trent Road, Bletchley in 1964. (Irene Smith – Winslow)

'My mother, knowing that I had two long walks in uncomfortable shoes, watched from her bedroom window, for as far as she could see, as I set off that first morning. Each day of that week, she watched, her heart becoming heavier, as my feet became red and sore and in need of plasters.

'On the Friday, as I was approaching the bus stop, an older girl, who had even further to walk because she went by our house on her way, was rushing to try and catch me up. Puffing and panting she explained, "Your mother sent these", and held out an old pair of plimsolls and a bag. Mother's message was "Do not worry about what these look like. No one will notice. Put them on to do your walking, carry your shoes in the bag and change when you get there."

'Grammar school was a very big step, but I had loving support on my journey!'

(Janet Rickard – Wingrave)

WINTER AND SUMMER

'Cold classrooms, one large coal fire in the front. We had to have our coats on in the back of the class. It was so cold the frozen milk bottles for break-time were put in the grate to defrost by the roaring fire. Our straws danced in the ice at the bottom of the bottle,' shivered *Pamela Allen (Winslow).*

Pat Heath (Downley Village Evening) went to West Wycombe school. 'I and another girl were monitors in the infants class and each day had to hand out and later collect small slate boards, which were used to write on instead of books. Round the walls were the times tables, made up with the paper gollies from the Robertson's jam jars. Winters were cold – one turtle stove per room, chafed legs, and being made to go into the playground in all weathers. During the summer we went on nature walks, had paperchase afternoons all over West Wycombe hill, and also picked hips and blackberries in season to help the post-war effort.'

CHAPTER NINE
HAVING FUN

*'We didn't have life quite so easy as now, but we were happy
and enjoyed life as it was then.'*

(Mrs D. Bignell – Wingrave)

In the Forties and Fifties most villages still created their own social life, as
Lindsey Haubner recalls for Coleshill.

'The old village hall or Parish Room was used like a clubhouse with darts,
billiards and cards played every night. No alcoholic drinks were served. Once
a month a large carpet was pulled out and rolled flat for the Women's Institute
meetings. Our Institute was founded in 1949. A big open fire would be lit in
the winter to warm the hall.

'There was always plenty of activity in the village. Regular dances and
whist drives in the Village hall, a successful football team, which is no
longer with us, and a cricket team which still is, although no longer entirely
made up of Coleshill players as it then was. Sport was only played on
Saturdays as Sunday was for church or chapel. The Brownies and Guides
first met in the downstairs part of the Windmill before moving into the
Village Hall. These, sadly, both finished in the 1990s when no one could be
found to run them.

'The Coronation of Queen Elizabeth II in 1953 was celebrated with a tea party
and all the children were given a Coronation mug. Rationing meant that there
were still very few sweets or special foods available.'

Hilary and Catherine Cross at the Chalfont St Peter Feast Day in 1956.
(Janet Cross – Horn Hill)

When we weren't at the pictures, we were
reading about them.

A CHRISTMAS CUSTOM

Beryl Hulbert found a touching custom being enacted at Oakley in the early Sixties when she first moved there.

'I remember being so surprised our first Christmas – one morning just before the schoolchildren broke up I heard a loud bell clanging outside, and on going to the gate saw a most beautifully decorated horse and cart driven by Father Christmas, with several small children seated beside him, coming down the road. They stopped at the home of each old age pensioner and, hand in hand with Father Christmas, one child carefully took a decorated box of goodies (2 lb sugar, 1 lb tea, apples, jelly, baked beans, chocolate bar etc) and a home-made, hand painted Christmas card to each door. The children at the village school still fundraise all year to pay for the items, bought in our local village shop, and this lovely custom continues today – but not with a horse and cart.'

FILM FUN

The cinema was still our favourite destination for a night out. *Pamela Allen (Winslow)* would be ready and waiting on Sunday afternoons in the Fifties:

'The Odeon in Aylesbury was our local cinema. On Sundays at 3.30 pm the Red Rover bus would arrive at the top of Station Road in Winslow from Buckingham, usually full up. If it was, we would get on the relief one, a double decker which started from Winslow. Both buses would leave some people standing at bus stops as they neared Aylesbury as both would be full by then.

'Two films and a trailer, and a cartoon, and we could sit through them twice if we wanted to.

'Afterwards we would go to the Kingsbury Square cafe and have egg, bacon and chips, tea and bread and butter.'

THE LAST BUS

'Teenagers' had only just been invented in the Fifties and certainly didn't have the freedom today's youngsters take for granted. Janet Rickard from Wingrave also wanted to go to the pictures in Aylesbury, but it wasn't quite so easy for her:

*We had to look our best for a night out – Amami and
'Mr Teazie Weazie' were famous names of their day.*

Your favourite Wave Set now has an exciting beauty extra

Amami *Wave Set*
and **CONDITIONER**

Amami Wave Set now contains a magic Conditioner. The Wave Set gives you glamorous waves and curls. The Conditioner gives them satin shine and softness, takes out all tangles, makes your set last longer—days longer. It encourages curl, grooms away wisps and frizz, settles new perms, strengthens old ones. Here's thrilling new beauty for every type of hair! Try it today. *Handy flasks* 1/4½ *and large economy size* 2/7½.

AMAMI GREEN
for hair that can be difficult.

AMAMI AMBER
for easier-to-manage hair.

More women by far use Amami Wave Set than any other Setting Lotion

royds AW24/20

'In the 1950s, when in our "late teens", to manage a visit to the Odeon in Aylesbury was quite an achievement. The question to one's parents sounded so simple and straightforward: "Please may I go to the pictures this week?"'

'The counter questions never seemed to be quite so simple. Why? Where? When? For how long? With whom? The answers needed to be convincing!'

'The film was one "not to be missed", we replied, everyone else was going, the friend or friends we were to be with were beyond reproach, in on one bus and out on another, all the other parents felt the film to be suitable...

'Permission granted. Plain sailing from now on ... Well?

'In this day and age it is difficult to comprehend, but we now needed to persuade our friends that we must enter the picture-house really early. No, not to get a good seat but in order to see the end of the film first!

The 'hit parade' was a selling point by 1958, though the record he is holding is still a 78 rpm!

'The last bus in our direction left the town at 10.15 pm, but the film did not end until later than that so if you did not see the last 20 minutes or so of the film first, you would never know the ending.

'Can you imagine the latter part of the film, how we sat on the edge of the seat, belongings in hand, all ready to creep out in the dark to leave the cinema and race to the bus stop to make sure we were all aboard the last bus home.'

A SOCIAL EVIL?

Well, it had to come! Our first experience of television is likely to have made a lasting impression, as *Irene Smith (Winslow)* recalls.

'It will be a social evil, declared Malcolm Muggeridge lugubriously. In 1949 I had yet to experience television.

'Then, with other children, I was invited by a kind couple to view their set. Smashing!

'We walked reverently into their lounge and sat the advised distance from the console set which had a shuttered screen. These shutters were opened, the room curtains were drawn and the television set switched on. We were amazed and fascinated.

Here comes Muffin, Muffin the Mule,
Dear old Muffin, playing the fool

sang Annette Mills at the piano while her marionette danced. Prudence Kitten, a glove puppet, looked on and purred.

'And so did we.'

ENTERTAINMENT TO THE FORE

Remember sheet music? And 78 rpm records? *June Mapley (Water Eaton)* started her working life in 1944 at Weatherheads Radio and Electrical shop in Bletchley.

'The lady in charge at that time was Brenda Healey, nee Underwood, and we still remain close friends. Accumulators were still in use for wireless sets, and because of our connection through them with acid we were allowed extra

Portable music in 1958.

clothing coupons. Trade was very busy with records and sheet music, with many of our customers from Bletchley Park. Bing Crosby, Frank Sinatra and classical records were very popular. A radiogram was at hand for customers to try records before purchase.

'In the early days after the war, not many people had televisions, so, when Princess Elizabeth was married in 1947, our shop was crowded with people watching the ceremony. In the late 1940s, Mr Bert Weatherhead and Mr Fred Higgs, with their wives and friends, attended a ball held at the Royal Albert Hall in London. This was to be televised, so I and several staff watched the event and, to our joy, the first couple to appear on screen were Mr and Mrs Higgs, dancing.

'During my teenage years, I attended the Baptist church in Aylesbury Street, later becoming Sunday school teacher and a member of the choir. With all the concerts and fetes, we had a very enjoyable time.

'In the Fifties and Sixties, entertainment in Bletchley was very much to the fore, with many concerts and dances held at Wilton Hall. I remember one very special one – *Carousel*, when Ray Ward sang My Little Girl. Coronation Hall in Water Eaton was also very popular, with many activities. We always had a very enjoyable New Year's Eve!'